MEDITATION

The First and Last Freedom

OSHO

MEDITATION
The First and Last Freedom

Published by OSHO Media International, 17 Koregaon Park, Pune 411001 MS, India

The excerpts in this book are taken from various OSHO Talks. All of these have been published in full as books and ebooks and are also available as original audio recordings. Audio recordings and the complete text archive can be found at osho.com/library

Printed in India by Parksons Graphics, Mumbai

ISBN 978-81-7261-239-9

This title is also available as an ebook: ISBN 978-0-88050-772-1

MEDICAL DISCLAIMER:
None of the methods in this book are intended to replace the services of a physician, therapist, or psychiatrist. Nor is the book meant to provide an alternative to professional medical treatment. This book offers no medical diagnosis of, or treatment for, any specific medical or psychological problem you may have. Some of the meditations include strenuous physical activity – if you have any reason to be concerned about the effects of such activity on your health, you should consult your physician before doing them.

TABLE OF CONTENTS

INTRODUCTION

Everyone knows that feeling: you arrive home and realize you have no memory of the journey. You made it back perfectly, on automatic pilot, while you were also engrossed in a kind of daydream or trance. Like you were transported into an imaginary movie happening somewhere else. Research suggests that we humans spend about half our waking hours in such "absent" spaces. Even stranger is that the same research shows we consistently report that we are happier when present than absent, irrespective of how much our minds tell us we dislike the task we are involved with.

Half our waking hours? That's half a lifetime! Imagine going to the doctor and being told that your current condition is cutting your life span in half. And you are worried about your salt intake?

Isn't it interesting how often in our lives people remind us to turn up for this meeting, or that event, or how we shouldn't miss this movie or that book. It's been going on forever: reminders to turn up for school, for work, for church, for the friend's wedding... Yet no one ever reminds us to turn up for our own lives.

It would be okay to miss the odd friend's wedding, but our life? And be less happy in the process? Now that is a bizarre situation for an otherwise pretty smart species like ours. Perhaps it is not so surprising that the planet Earth is such a mess, when we realize that there are seven billion of us running around on automatic pilot half the time.

Do any of us really doubt that things tend to go better when we turn up? Whether it is struggling with our tax returns or going for a walk with our best friend – it kind of helps to be there!

You have to wonder what this is all about. Seems we are operating on a version of hardware/software that was designed for one world, while trying to live in another. Maybe that's just it. We have just emerged from a fairly rough few million years since we came down from the trees. Forget the salt intake, for most of that time we were happy just to avoid being some wild animal's intake! And for almost all this time we have had to hunt for our best meals. Now the only hunting we do is to scratch around for our credit card.

So, we seven billion, part-time sleepwalkers are messing up ourselves, each other, and the planet. And because we are half asleep, we don't even notice what is happening, let alone realize that we are not even enjoying it! Eventually someone had to notice. And when people looked into it, they discovered that the essence of being present and awake is what meditation is all about.

For the contemporary, post-modern people it was a natural. They are already more interested in the quality of their lives rather than the quantity of stuff in their lives. They are more open to the feminine, to patience, and regard the old patriarchal values as primitive. They are already less interested in outer authority, whether it is religion or science, but look inside for what is right for them. They want to customize their lives for themselves; they are not mass-produced sheep looking for a shepherd. For these people, life is an art in itself, not a means to some who-knows-what.

Then the academics noticed. All the best schools in the US have departments discovering that meditators age more slowly, have less stress, are healthier, are more considerate of others, make better leaders, are more creative, more productive... On top of that, they also discovered that the brain is a plastic organ. It is like a computer that changes depending how you use it. It is up to you!

Then the people who pay the bills noticed. More productive did you say? If you are paying someone to turn up to work and he or she is off in a daydream for half the day, that can get your attention. And what about my own productivity? Wouldn't it make sense to actually be present for whatever I am trying to do? And did you mention stress and health? Two-thirds of visits to doctors are for stress-related complaints. Then all the days missed at work... That's a cool 300 billion dollars right there. Not to mention the suffering.

Or put another way: would an engaged, enthusiastic, healthy workforce be good for them and good for the company, and good for the community in general? It is not surprising that companies everywhere are moving in this direction: already a quarter of US companies are offering some kind of stress reduction program. They are beginning to realize that companies that don't do well by their employees are not doing well. Period.

So, whether you care about you, your neighbors, or the world around you, meditation would be the place to start. Okay, so at least give it a shot.

Before you rush off into "meditation" there are one or two other major points to consider. Modern people are not the same as the people for whom "just sitting" worked well in the past. We are starting from a very different place. We live in a supercomplex, sophisticated world of interacting ideas and emotions – a different planet from the simple village life of the early meditators. Fact is, we are emotionally loaded. No wonder the main mindfulness meditation teachers are noticing that just sitting doesn't work for many people. And may not work totally for anyone. Simply put: you cannot expect to relax if you are sitting on a volcano.

That is why you will find in this book a wide variety of active meditations that give you the opportunity to really let go, to let off steam. Then sit still and see the difference.

Finally, you will also notice that the Osho approach to meditation includes many body-based or movement-based meditations, often incorporating dancing. We all pay lip service these days to the unitary nature of the mind and body. Deep down we usually mean that the mind is really the boss but the body shouldn't be ignored. The latest scientific approach suggests that, rather than the body being mainly there to provide room service for the mind – so it can do all those wonderful things like thinking and dreaming and being anywhere but present – it may be the opposite. The function of the mind is now said to ensure that the body moves in the most intelligent way possible. The mind as a servant of the body.

What that means is that, instead of having to struggle with the mind because it just won't change and keeps up the same old routine, start with the body. You know how easy it is to tell from someone's body language whether they are happy or depressed for example. Well, in exactly the same way, when the body changes, the mind will change too. Moving the body is so much easier than moving the mind! And much more fun too.

As Osho puts it:

"Meditation has become something absolutely needed, the only hope for humanity to be saved, for the earth to still remain alive. Meditation simply means the capacity to get involved yet remain unattached. It looks paradoxical – all great truths are paradoxical. You have to experience the paradox; that is the only way to understand it. You can do a thing joyously and yet just be a witness that you are doing it, that you are not the doer.

Try with small things, and you will understand. Tomorrow when you go for a morning walk, enjoy the walk – the birds in the trees and the sunrays and the clouds and the wind. Enjoy, and still remember that you are a mirror; you are reflecting the clouds and the trees and the birds and the people.

This self-remembering, Buddha calls sammasati, right mindfulness. Krishnamurti calls it choiceless awareness, the Upanishads call it witnessing, Gurdjieff calls it self-remembering, but they all mean the same. But it does not mean that you have to become indifferent; if you become indifferent you lose the opportunity to self-remember.

Go on a morning walk and still remember that you are not it – you are not the walker but the watcher. And slowly, slowly you will have the taste of it – it is a taste, it comes slowly. And it is the most delicate phenomenon in the world; you cannot get it in a hurry. Patience is needed.

Eat, taste the food, and still remember that you are the watcher. In the beginning it will create a little trouble in you because you have not done these two things together. In the beginning, I know if you start watching, you will feel like stopping eating, or if you start eating you will forget watching.

Our consciousness is one-way – right now, as it is – it goes only toward the target. But it can become two-way – it can eat and yet watch. You can remain settled in your center and you can see the storm around you; you can become the center of the cyclone. And that is the greatest miracle that can happen to a human being, because that brings freedom, liberation, truth, godliness, bliss, benediction."

John Andrews M.D. M.R.C.P.

PREFACE TO THE NEW EDITION

What this book is about

This is a practical meditation handbook and a support to introduce the reader to Osho's meditations. It is a selection of what Osho has to share in his many talks about the process of entering into and deepening meditation. Some of the techniques presented here require setting time aside, while others integrate meditation into your day-to-day activities.

When the first edition of this book was completed, Osho supported it to become his main meditation handbook. The book includes a large variety of meditation techniques, some of which Osho developed literally until his last day on this planet. It has become one of Osho's most popular books and has already been translated into more than 30 languages.

What's changed

In this new edition you will find meditations that were not previously included, some of which were developed after the first edition was published. Of particular significance is the OSHO Evening Meeting Meditation, which is the highlight of the day at the OSHO International Meditation Resort. It is a meditation that Osho recommends for everyone interested in his methods.

The first edition contained many meditations from Osho's *The Book of Secrets*, in which Osho made the 112 ancient meditation methods of the *Vigyan Bhairav Tantra* accessible for modern man. Now that *The Book of Secrets* has become a worldwide success in its own right, and is available in many languages, we have reduced some of that previous content in this new edition of *Meditation: The First and Last Freedom*. This has enabled us to bring in additional meditations from other Osho sources.

Over the last years, Osho International Foundation has undertaken the global project of going back to the original audio sources and checking the recordings and earlier editing.

This has made it possible to correct and update cited texts. Previously unpublished texts have become available and new additional material has been introduced to some of the meditations, particularly from the expanded effort to translate Osho's Hindi talks.

We have responded to feedback and questions from meditators and from the spread of Osho meditation facilitators around the world. We have also analyzed the topics searched for in osho.com. This has led to an expanded chapter, "Letting Go, Death and Dying," the addition of a new chapter, "Children and Meditation," and a section on the use of specific music for various meditation techniques. Looking at current lifestyle issues in the media has led to adding a meditation technique on eating, an expanded section on physical work and exercise, and a new chapter, "Dealing with Feelings."

Other additions provide enhanced recognition of Osho's unique contribution not only in the creation of his OSHO Active Meditations and OSHO Meditative Therapies, but also in areas such as his recognition of laughter and celebration as important meditation tools and spiritual qualities.

The use of Osho's words and editorial text

The text set in Roman type indicates that these are direct quotations from Osho's collected works. The meditation instructions and any editorial texts are printed in italics – although even these texts include Osho's own expressions as far as possible. Very occasionally in the instructions his words have been put into quotation marks for emphasis.

How to use this book

The text has been divided into two main parts. The first part is *about* meditation, and the second contains the meditations themselves. You can read the content of these parts in any order, or move back and forth, according to your preference.

As you explore this book, experiment with the meditations that appeal to you at this time – and continue for a few days. As Osho says:

"We need methods that yield quick results. If a man makes a seven-day commitment, by the end of that period he should begin to feel that something has happened to him. He should become a different man in seven days' time... So, I say, practice today and feel the result immediately."

When you feel that you have found your method, continue to practice it until you feel complete with it. Then there will be another method waiting that will click with you for your continuing journey.

Whatever the activity – and there are so many possibilities to experiment with in this book – Osho always comes back to the process of awareness, of witnessing.

PART I

ABOUT MEDITATION

1

WHAT IS MEDITATION?

Watching is meditation. What you watch is irrelevant. You can watch the trees, you can watch the river, you can watch the clouds, you can watch children playing around. Watching is meditation. What you watch is not the point; the object is not the point. The quality of observation, the quality of being aware and alert – that's what meditation is.

Remember one thing: meditation means awareness. Whatsoever you do with awareness is meditation. The action is not the question, but the quality that you bring to your action. Walking can be a meditation, if you walk alertly. Sitting can be a meditation, if you sit alertly. Listening to the birds can be a meditation, if you listen with awareness. Just listening to the inner noise of your mind can be a meditation, if you remain alert and watchful. The whole point is: one should not move in sleep. Then whatsoever you do is meditation.

When you are not doing anything at all – bodily, mentally, on any level – when all activity has ceased and you simply are, just being, that's what meditation is. You cannot do it, you cannot practice it; you have only to understand it.

Whenever you can find time for just being and drop all doing… Thinking is also doing, concentration is also doing, contemplation is also doing. If even for a single moment you are not doing anything and you are just at your center, utterly relaxed – that is meditation. And once you have the knack of it, you can remain in that state as long as you want; finally you can remain in that state twenty-four hours a day.

Once you have become aware of the way "just being" can remain undisturbed, then slowly you can start doing things, keeping alert that being is not stirred. That is the second part of meditation. First, learning how just to be, and then learning little actions: cleaning the floor, taking a shower, but keeping yourself centered. Then you can do complicated things.

For example, I am speaking to you, but my meditation is not disturbed. I can go on speaking, but at my very center there is not even a ripple; it is just silent, utterly silent.

So meditation is not against action. It is not that you have to escape from life. It simply teaches you a new way of life: you become the center of a cyclone.

Your life goes on, it goes on really more intensely – with more joy, with more clarity, more vision, more creativity – yet you are aloof, just a watcher on the hills, simply seeing all that is happening around you.

You are not the doer, you are the watcher.

That's the whole secret of meditation: you become the watcher. Doing continues on its own level, there is no problem: chopping wood, drawing water from the well. You can do all the small and big things; only one thing is not allowed and that is your centering should not be lost.

That awareness, that watchfulness, should remain absolutely unclouded, undisturbed.

In Judaism there is a rebellious mystery school called Hasidism. Its founder, Baal Shem, was a rare being. In the middle of the night he was coming back from the river – that was his routine, because at the river in the night it was absolutely calm and quiet. And he used to simply sit there, doing nothing – just watching his own self, watching the watcher.

This night, when he was coming back, he passed a rich man's house and the watchman was standing by the door. The watchman was puzzled because every night, at exactly this time, he would come by. The watchman came out and said, "Forgive me for interrupting, but I cannot contain my curiosity anymore. You are haunting me day and night, every day. What is your business? Why do you go to the river? I have followed you many times and there is nothing – you simply sit there for hours and then in the middle of the night you come back."

Baal Shem said, "I know that you have followed me many times, because the night is so silent I can hear your footsteps. And I know you are hiding behind the gate every day. But it is not only that you are curious about me, I am also curious about you. What is your business?"

He said, "My business? I am a simple watchman."

Baal Shem said, "My God, you have given me the key word. This is my business too!"

The watchman said, "But I don't understand. If you are a watchman you should be watching some house, some palace. What are you watching there, sitting in the sand?"

Baal Shem said, "There is a little difference: you are watching for somebody outside who may enter the palace; I simply watch this watcher. Who is this watcher? This is my whole life's effort; I watch myself."

The watchman said, "But this is a strange business. Who is going to pay you?"

He said, "It is such bliss, such a joy, such immense benediction, it pays itself profoundly. Just a single moment, and all the treasures are nothing in comparison to it."

The watchman said, "This is strange; I have been watching my whole life. I never came across such a beautiful experience. Tomorrow night I am coming with you. Just teach me. I know how to watch – it seems only a different direction is needed; you are watching in a different direction."

There is only one step, and that step is of direction, of dimension. Either we can be focused outside or we can close our eyes to the outside and let our whole consciousness be centered within. And you will know, because you are a knower, you are awareness. You have never lost it, you simply entangled your awareness in a thousand and one things. Withdraw your awareness from everywhere and just let it rest within yourself, and you have arrived home.

—

The mind is a shadow existence, as if one is looking in a mirror and starts thinking "I am inside the mirror." You are not inside the mirror; the mirror is reflecting something that is confronting the mirror. The mind is a mirror, a beautiful mirror, very useful, but it is very easy to get caught in it because you don't know yourself, and whatsoever you know about yourself, you know from the mind. You only know your face because of the mirror; the mirror becomes very important. And all that one knows through the mind is a reflection, it is not real. The real has to be known without the mind; the mind has to be put aside. One has to face oneself immediately, without the mind. And that's all, the whole science of meditation: how to put the mind aside, how to be mindless for a few moments.

In the beginning they are very tiny moments, just drops of mindlessness, but immensely illuminating, immensely transforming. If even a drop of mindlessness enters your being, you have tasted something of the reality. And that taste lingers on your tongue forever, you cannot forget it.

Only after that taste can you see that the mind is just reflecting things, because now you can compare. Without that experience there is no way to compare. With what to compare? You know all that the mind says to you, and it is all from the mind. Something has to be known that is not from the mind and then you will see that the mind starts becoming pale. Then you know that the reality is totally different, utterly different.

So this has to be done, and it can be done. The mind is not a must; it can be put aside. It is an activity – it can be put to rest. It is like walking: when you need to walk, you walk; when you don't need, you put your legs to rest. The mind is an activity, more subtle than walking, but there is no need for it to continue twenty-four hours a day. When it is needed, use it; it is a biocomputer, immensely helpful in work. But when it is not needed, put it aside, tell it to slow down, tell it to go to sleep and rest.

In the beginning, it will not listen because for so many lives you have been listening to it. The servant has become the master and the master has been behaving like a servant. So right now it is not going to listen if you say "Stop!" But if you go on, slowly, slowly the master begins his mastery and the servant starts behaving. The mind is beautiful as a servant but it is very evil as a master. When you are the master and the mind follows you like a servant, it is a beautiful instrument, a great mechanism to be used. It can be helpful in many ways, but only as a servant.

⁓

The first step in awareness is to be very watchful of your body. Slowly, slowly one becomes alert about each gesture, each movement. And as you become aware, a miracle starts happening: many things that you used to do before simply disappear, your body becomes more relaxed, your body becomes more attuned. A deep peace starts prevailing even in your body, a subtle music pulsates in your body.

Then start becoming aware of your thoughts: the same has to be done with thoughts. They are more subtle than the body and, of course, more dangerous too. And when you become aware of your thoughts, you will be surprised what goes on inside you. If you write down whatsoever is going on at any moment, you are in for a great surprise. You will not believe what is going on inside you.

Just for ten minutes go on writing. Close the doors, lock the doors and windows so nobody can come in and you can be totally honest. Later you can throw it in the fire, so nobody will know except you! And then be truly honest; go on writing whatsoever is going on inside the mind. Don't interpret it, don't change it, don't edit it. Just put it on the paper as naked as it is, exactly as it is.

After ten minutes, read it – you will see a mad mind inside! Because we are not aware, this whole madness goes on running like an undercurrent. It affects whatsoever you are doing, it affects whatsoever you are not doing; it affects everything. And the sum total of it is going to be your life! So this madman has to be changed. And the miracle of awareness is that you need not do anything *except* just become aware.

The very phenomenon of watching it changes it. Slowly, slowly the madman disappears; slowly, slowly the thoughts start falling into a certain pattern; their chaos is no more, they become more of a cosmos. And then again a deeper peace prevails. When your body and your mind are at peace you will see that they are attuned to each other too, there is a bridge. Now they are not running in different directions, they are not riding different horses. For the first time there is accord, and that accord helps immensely to work on the third step – that is, becoming aware of your feelings, emotions, moods.

That is the subtlest layer and the most difficult, but if you can be aware of the thoughts then it is just one more step. A little more intense awareness is needed and you start reflecting your moods, your emotions, your feelings. Once you are aware of the body, the mind, and the emotions, they all become joined into one phenomenon. And when all three are one – functioning together perfectly, humming together, you can feel the music of all three; they have become an orchestra – then the fourth happens, which you cannot do. It happens on its own accord. It is a gift from the whole, it is a reward for those who have done these three.

The fourth is the ultimate awareness that makes one awakened. One becomes aware of one's awareness – that is the fourth. That makes a buddha, the awakened. And only in that awakening does one come to know what bliss is. The body knows pleasure, the mind knows happiness, the heart knows joy, the fourth knows bliss. Bliss is the goal of sannyas, of being a seeker, and awareness is the path toward it.

Meditation is going beyond time. Time is mind. The mind consists of past and future; it has no experience of the present. It is thought that time has three tenses: past, present and future. I don't agree, my own experience is totally different: time consists only of two tenses, past and future. The present is not part of time, the present is part of eternity. It is a totally different thing. Past and future are horizontal and present is vertical.

The mind lives horizontally, meditation is a vertical phenomenon. When you drop out of the past and the future, suddenly you enter the present and that is beyond time. That is the beginning of godliness, of truth, the beginning of that which is.

The whole science of meditation is to help you to get rid of past and future; and in fact it is not much of a task because the past is no longer and the future is not yet, so you are simply getting rid of something which is not yet – it is not much of a task. And you are getting rid of something which is no more – that too is not much of a task. You are entering that which is and which always is. Hence meditation is simple, just the right understanding is needed.

But in the name of meditation, so many stupidities go on in the world that people have become very confused: What is meditation? People are chanting mantras, doing certain rituals, worshipping, bowing down to statues. All kinds of things are being done. The Tibetan Buddhists go on doing things the whole day: lying down on the ground and touching the ground with their heads. And the more you do it, the more meditative you become. There are people who do it one thousand times a day, two thousand times a day, three thousand times a day – the bigger the number, the greater you are. And just think, a person doing this nonsense of lying down on the earth and touching the earth with his head for the whole day – of course he will become mindless... But that is not meditation. That is falling below mind, not going above mind. He will become idiotic but he will not become a buddha. He may become very robust because it is a good exercise, continuously doing it for the whole day. He may enjoy good health, but he will be utterly in an illusion if he thinks that he knows what meditation is.

Then people are continuously chanting mantras – they become mechanical, they go on chanting and they go on thinking also. Mind is capable of doing many things, you just have to learn the trick. You can try it – you can chant "Rama, Rama, Rama, Rama..." and after a few days start counting, "One, two, three, four. One, two, three, four, Rama, Rama. One, two, three, four, Rama..." and both will start happening together. You will have both together. "Rama, Rama and one, two, three, four," then a woman passes by and you look and you miss and that too enters the head and you start fighting, feeling "This is not good."

The mind is capable of many processes together, so you cannot get rid of it just by chanting a mantra. All that is needed is a great understanding, awareness, alertness, not to go into past memories and not to get into trips about the future.

Slowly, slowly one settles in the present. The moment you are here-now you have found it.

2

MISUNDERSTANDINGS
ABOUT MEDITATION

Even a meditation can be wrong. People have a wrong notion that all meditations are right. It is not so. Meditations can be wrong. For example, any meditation that leads you deep into concentration is wrong and it will not result in compassion. You will become more and more closed rather than becoming open. If you narrow down your consciousness, if you concentrate on something and you exclude the whole of existence and become one-pointed, it will create more and more tension in you. Hence the word *attention*: it means "a tension." *Concentration*, the very sound of the word, gives you a feeling of tenseness.

Concentration has its uses, but it is not meditation. In scientific work, in scientific research, in the science lab, you need concentration. You have to concentrate on one problem and exclude everything else – so much so that you become almost unmindful of the remaining world. The one problem that you are concentrating upon is your world. That's why scientists become absentminded. People who concentrate too much always become absentminded because they don't know how to remain open to the whole world.

I was reading an anecdote:

"I have brought a frog," said a scientist, a professor of zoology, beaming at his class, "fresh from the pond, in order that we might study its outer appearance and later dissect it."

He carefully unwrapped the package he carried and inside was a neatly prepared ham sandwich. The good professor looked at it with astonishment.

"Odd!" he said, "I distinctly remember having eaten my lunch."

That goes on happening to scientists: they become one-pointed and the whole mind becomes narrow. Of course, a narrow mind has its use: it becomes more penetrating, it becomes like a sharp needle, it hits exactly the right point – but it misses the great life that surrounds you.

A buddha is not a man of concentration, he is a man of awareness. He has not been trying to narrow down his consciousness; on the contrary, he has been trying to drop all barriers so that he becomes totally available to existence. Watch: existence is simultaneous. I am speaking here and the traffic noise is simultaneous, the train, the birds, the wind blowing through the trees; in this moment, the whole of existence converges. You listening to me, I speaking to you, and millions of things are going on – it is tremendously rich. Concentration makes you one-pointed at a very great cost: ninety-nine percent of life is discarded. Let me tell you a few basic things. One, meditation is not concentration but relaxation. One simply relaxes. One simply relaxes into oneself. The more you relax, the more you feel yourself open, vulnerable. The more you relax, the less rigid you are; you become more flexible and suddenly existence starts penetrating you. You are no longer like a rock, you have openings. Relaxation means allowing yourself to fall into a state where you are not doing anything, because if you are doing something, tension will continue. It is a state of non-doing: you simply relax and enjoy the feeling of relaxation.

Relax into yourself. Just close your eyes and listen to all that is happening all around – no need to feel anything as a distraction. The moment you feel it is a distraction, you are denying existence. This moment existence has come to you as a bird – don't deny it. It has knocked at your door as a bird. The next moment it has come as a dog barking, or as a child crying and weeping, or as a madman laughing. Don't deny it, don't reject it, accept – because if you deny you will become tense. All denials create tension. Accept. If you want to relax, acceptance is the way. Accept whatsoever is happening all around, let it become an organic whole. It is! You may know it, you may not know it, but everything is interrelated. These birds, these trees, this sky, this sun, this earth, you, me, all are related. It is an organic unity. If the sun disappears, the trees will disappear; if the trees disappear, the birds will disappear; if the birds and trees disappear, you cannot be here, you will disappear. It is an ecology: everything is deeply related with everything else.

So don't deny anything because the moment you deny, you are denying something in you. If you deny these singing birds, then something in you is denied.

And when I say watch, don't try to watch; otherwise you will become tense again and you will start concentrating on the breath. Simply relax, remain relaxed, loose. And look – because what else can you do? You are there, nothing to be done, everything accepted, nothing to be denied, rejected, no struggle, no fight, no conflict, breathing going deep – what can you do? Simply watch.

Introspection is thinking about yourself. Self-remembering is not thinking at all: it is becoming aware about yourself. The difference is subtle, but very great. Western psychology insists on introspection, and Eastern psychology insists on self-remembering. When you introspect, what do you do? For example, you are angry: you start thinking about anger – how it is caused. You start analyzing why it is caused. You start judging whether it is good or bad. You start rationalizing that you had been angry because the situation was such. You brood about the anger, you analyze the anger, but the focus of attention is on the anger, not on the self. Your whole consciousness is focused on the anger – you are watching, analyzing, associating, thinking about it, thinking how to avoid it, how to get rid of it, how not to do it again. This is a thinking process. You will judge it "bad" because it is destructive. You will take a vow: "I will never commit the same mistake again." You will try to control this anger through will. That's why Western psychology has become analytical; it is analysis, dissection.

The Eastern emphasis is not on the anger. The Eastern emphasis is on the self. To be aware when you are angry, to be so aware... Not to think, because thinking is a sleeping thing. You can think while you are fast asleep; there is no need for awareness. In fact, you continuously think without being at all aware. The thinking goes on and on and on. Even when you are fast asleep at night, the thinking continues, the mind goes on continuing its inner chatter. It is a mechanical thing.

Eastern psychology says, "Be aware. Don't try to analyze anger, there is no need. Just look at it, but look with awareness. Don't start thinking." In fact, if you start thinking then thinking will become a barrier to looking at anger. Then thinking will garb it. Then thinking will be like a cloud surrounding it; the clarity will be lost. Don't think at all. Be in a state of no-thought, and *look*.

When there is not even a ripple of thinking between you and the anger, the anger is faced, encountered. You don't dissect it.

You don't bother to go to its source because the source is in the past. You don't judge it because the moment you judge, thinking starts. You don't take a vow that "I will not do it" because that vow leads you into the future. In awareness you remain with the feeling of anger – exactly here-now. You are not interested in changing it, you are not interested in thinking about it – you are interested in looking at it directly, face-to-face, immediate. Then it is self-remembering.

And this is the beauty of it: if you can look at anger it disappears. It not only disappears in that moment; the very disappearance of it by your deep look gives you the key – there is no need to use will, there is no need to make any decision for the future, and there is no need to go to the original source from which it comes. It is unnecessary. You have the key now: look at anger, and the anger disappears. And this look is available forever. Whenever anger is there you can look; then this looking grows deeper.

There are three stages of looking. First, when the anger has already happened and gone; as if you look at a tail disappearing – an elephant has gone; only the tail is there. When the anger was there, you were so deeply involved in it you could not really be aware. When the anger has almost disappeared, ninety-nine percent gone – only one percent, the last part of it is going, disappearing into the horizon – then you become aware. This is the first state of awareness – good, but not enough.

The second state is when the elephant is there – not the tail – when the situation is ripe. You are really angry to the peak, boiling, burning – then you become aware.

Then there is still a third stage: the anger has not yet come, is still coming – not the tail but the head. It is just entering your area of consciousness and you become aware, then the elephant never materializes. You killed the animal before it was born. That is birth control! The phenomenon has not happened; then it leaves no trace.

3

SOME BENEFITS
OF MEDITATION

These are the ways and the criteria of how one has to choose. If you move on any path – any methodology – and it brings you more sensitivity, more watchfulness, and gives a feeling of immense well-being, this is the only criterion that you are going on the right path. If you become more miserable, more angry, more of an egoist, more greedy, more lustful, those are the indications you are moving on a wrong path.

On the right path your blissfulness is going to grow more and more every day.

It is your very nature to be blissful. Meditation gives you only that which you have always had. It simply makes you aware of your reality. It does not bring anything new in. It simply reveals to you the treasure that is lying there ignored and neglected, while you are running all over the world for it. You will not find it anywhere else because it is within you.

Silence

Silence is usually understood to be something negative, something empty: an absence of sound, of noise. This misunderstanding is prevalent because very few people have ever experienced silence.

All that they have experienced in the name of silence is noiselessness. But silence is a totally different phenomenon. It is utterly positive. It is existential, it is not empty. It is overflowing with a music that you have never heard before, and with a fragrance that is unfamiliar to you, and with a light that can only be seen by the inner eyes.

It is not something fictitious; it is a reality, and a reality which is already present in everyone – we just never look in.

Your inner world has its own taste, has its own fragrance, has its own light. And it is utterly silent, immensely silent, eternally silent. There has never been any noise, and there will never be any noise. No word can reach there, but you can reach.

Your very center of being is the center of a cyclone. Whatever happens around it does not affect it. It is eternal silence: days come and go, years come and go, ages come and pass. Lives come and go, but the eternal silence of your being remains exactly the same – the same soundless music, the same fragrance of godliness, the same transcendence from all that is mortal, from all that is momentary.

It is not *your* silence. You *are* it.

It is not something in your possession; you are possessed by it, and that's the greatness of it. Even you are not there, because even your presence will be a disturbance.

The silence is so profound that there is nobody, not even you. And this silence brings truth, and love, and thousands of other blessings to you. This is the search, this is the longing of all the hearts, of all those who have a little intelligence.

Sensitivity

You become so sensitive that even the smallest blade of grass takes on an immense importance for you. Your sensitivity makes it clear to you that this small blade of grass is as important to existence as the biggest star; without this blade of grass, existence would be less than it is. This small blade of grass is unique, it is irreplaceable, it has its own individuality.

And this sensitivity will create new friendships for you – friendships with trees, with birds, with animals, with mountains, with rivers, with oceans, with stars. Life becomes richer as love grows, as friendliness grows.

Meditation will bring you sensitivity, a great sense of belonging to the world. It is our world – the stars are ours, and we are not foreigners here. We belong intrinsically to existence. We are part of it; we are the *heart* of it.

Love

If you meditate, sooner or later you will come upon love. If you meditate deeply, sooner or later you will start feeling a tremendous love arising in you that you have never known before – a new quality to your being, a new door opening. You have become a new flame and now you want to share.

If you love deeply, by and by you will become aware that your love is becoming more and more meditative. A subtle quality of silence is entering you. Thoughts are disappearing, gaps appearing – silences. You are touching your own depth.

Millions of couples around the world are living as if love is there. They are living in a world of "as if." Of course, how can they be joyous? They are drained of all energy, they are trying to get something out of a false love. It cannot deliver the goods, hence the frustration, hence the continuous boredom, hence the continuous nagging, fighting between the lovers. They both are trying to do something which is impossible; they are trying to make their love affair something of the eternal, which it cannot be. It has arisen out of the mind and the mind cannot give you any glimpse of the eternal.

First go into meditation, because love will come out of meditation. It is the fragrance of meditation.

Compassion
When your love is not just a desire for the other, when your love is not only a need, when your love is a sharing, when your love is not that of a beggar but that of an emperor, when your love is not asking for something in return but is ready just to give – to give for the sheer joy of giving – then add meditation to it and the pure fragrance is released, the imprisoned splendor is released. That is compassion; compassion is the highest phenomenon.

Sex is animal, love is human, compassion is divine. Sex is physical, love is psychological, compassion is spiritual.

Joy
For no reason at all, you suddenly feel joyous. In ordinary life, if there is a reason, you are joyful. You have met a beautiful woman and you are joyous, or you have the money that you always wanted and you are joyous, or you have purchased a house with a beautiful garden and you are joyous, but these joys cannot last long. They are momentary; they cannot remain continuous and uninterrupted.

If your joy is caused by something it will disappear, it will be momentary. It will soon leave you in deep sadness; all joys leave you in deep sadness. But there is a different kind of joy that is a confirmatory sign: you are suddenly joyous for no reason at all. You cannot pinpoint why. If somebody asks, "Why are you so joyous?" you cannot answer.

I cannot say why I am joyous. There is no reason. It's simply so. Now, *this* joy cannot be disturbed. Now whatsoever happens, it will continue. It is there, day in, day out. You may be young, you may be old, you may be alive, you may be dying – it is always there. When you have found a joy that remains – circumstances change but it abides – then you are certainly coming closer to buddhahood.

Intelligence

A great definition of meditation: intelligence is meditation. To live intelligently is to live meditatively. This definition is of tremendous significance; it is really pregnant with great meaning. To live intelligently is what meditation is. Meditation cannot be "done" in that way. You have to bring intelligence to your life.

You were angry yesterday, you were angry the day before yesterday. Now again the situation has come and you are going to be angry – what are you going to do? Are you going to repeat it in an unintelligent way, a mechanical way, or will you bring intelligence to it? You have been angry a thousand and one times – can't you learn anything from it? Can't you behave intelligently now? Can't you see the futility of it? Can't you see that you were frustrated by it every time? Each time anger has dissipated energy, distracted your energy, created problems for you, and not solved anything.

If you see it, in that very seeing is intelligence. Then somebody insults you and there is no anger. In fact, rather than anger there is compassion for the man. He is angry, he is hurt, he is suffering. Compassion will arise. Now, this intelligence is meditation: to look into one's life, to learn out of experience, to learn out of existential experience, to go on learning, not borrowing.

—

Intelligence simply means the ability to respond, because life is a flux. You have to be aware and to see what is demanded of you, what is the challenge of the situation. The intelligent person behaves according to the situation and the stupid behaves according to ready-made answers. Whether they come from Buddha, Christ or Krishna does not matter. He always carries scriptures around himself; he is afraid to depend on himself. The intelligent person depends on his own insight, he trusts his own being.

Aloneness

Meditation means: bliss in being alone.

One is *really* alive when one has become capable of that, when there is no dependence anymore on anybody, on any situation, on any condition. And because the bliss is one's own, it can remain morning, evening; day, night; in youth or in old age; in health, in illness. In life, in death too, it can remain because it is not something that is happening to you from the outside. It is something welling up in you. It is your very nature. It is self-nature.

Celebrate aloneness, celebrate your pure space, and a great song will arise in your heart. And it will be a song of awareness, it will be a song of meditation. It will be a song of a lone bird calling in the distance – not calling to somebody in particular, but just calling because the heart is full and wants to call, because the cloud is full and wants to rain, because the flower is full and the petals open and the fragrance is released, unaddressed. Let your aloneness become a dance.

Individuality

Meditation is nothing but a device to make you aware of your real self, which is not created by you, which need not be created by you, which you already are. You are born with it, you *are* it! It needs to be discovered.

Society does not allow it to happen; no society allows it to happen because the real self is dangerous, dangerous for the established church, dangerous for the state, dangerous for the crowd, dangerous for tradition, because once a man knows his real self he becomes an individual. He no longer belongs to the mob psychology; he will not be superstitious and he cannot be exploited. He cannot be led like cattle, he cannot be ordered and commanded. He will live according to his light, he will live from his own inwardness. His life will have tremendous beauty, integrity. But that is the fear of society.

Integrated people become individuals, and society wants you to be nonindividuals. Instead of individuality, society teaches you to be a personality. The word *personality* has to be understood. It comes from the root, *persona* – *persona* means "mask."

The society gives you a false idea of who you are; it gives you just a toy, and you go on clinging to the toy your whole life.

As I see it, almost everybody is in the wrong place. The person who would have been a tremendously happy doctor is a painter and the person who would have been a tremendously happy painter is a doctor. Nobody seems to be in his right place, and that's why this whole society is in such a mess. Each person is directed by others, he is not directed by his own intuition.

Meditation helps you to grow your own intuitive faculty. It becomes very clear what is going to fulfill you, what is going to help you flower. And whatsoever it is, is going to be different for each individual. That is the meaning of the word, *individual*: everybody is unique. And to seek and search your uniqueness is a great thrill, a great adventure.

Creativity

Meditation releases great creativity. It is an explosion; all your seeds start sprouting. For the first time, you see how much potential you were carrying within yourself: a great garden with so many flowers, such beautiful bushes and trees and so many birds singing... A whole paradise! But we are not ordinarily aware of it. We are completely closed, we have not opened up; we are living like a capsule which has no opening, no windows.

Leibniz has the right word for it. He calls man a monad, a windowless house: no doors, no windows. Meditation throws open all the doors and all the windows. Suddenly you become aware of the vast sky, the stars, the moon, the sun, the wind, the rain, the rainbows, the clouds – the whole infinity of it, the whole spectrum of it. And the moment you become aware of it, your heart starts singing and dancing.

To whatsoever you do, there is the golden touch of creativity.

4

THE SCIENCE
OF MEDITATION

Experiment

Natural evolution has stopped at man. This is a fact. Even scientists are becoming more and more aware of it: for thousands of years nothing has happened to man – he has remained the same, as if nature's work is done. Now man has to take the course of further growth into his own hands. That's what religion is.

Religion means that man starts standing on his own feet, becomes responsible for his own being, starts looking and searching and inquiring into: "Who am I?" And this should not only be curiosity.

Philosophy is out of curiosity. Religion is a very sincere, authentic search; it is inquiry. And there is a great difference between curiosity and inquiry. Curiosity is childish, just a little itching in the head. You would like to scratch and then you feel satisfied; philosophy is that scratching. Religion is a life-and-death matter. In philosophy you never become involved, you remain aloof. You play with the toys, but it is not a question of life and death. You accumulate knowledge, but you never practice it.

I have heard: Once upon a time there lived an eminent Confucian scholar. He was a gentleman of nearly eighty, and was said to have no equal in learning and understanding.

Then a rumor arose that far away a new doctrine had sprung up that was even deeper than his knowledge. The old gentleman found this intolerable and decided that the issue had to be settled one way or the other.

In spite of his age, he set out on the long journey. After months of hardship on the road, he arrived at his destination, introduced himself and told the purpose of his visit.

His host, who was a master of the new Zen school, merely quoted, "To avoid doing evil, to do as much good as possible, this is the teaching of all the buddhas."

On hearing this, the Confucian gentleman flared up: "I have come here in spite of the dangers and hazards of such a long and rough journey and in spite of my advanced age. And you just quote a little jingle that every three-year-old child knows by heart! Are you mocking me?"

But the Zen master replied, "I am not mocking you, sir. Please consider that, although it is true that every three-year-old child knows this verse, even a man of eighty fails to live up to it!" Religion is not a question of knowing, but of living up to it. Religion is life and unless you live it, you will not know anything about what it is. To live religion, one has to drop all philosophizing and one has to start experimenting. One has to become a lab. The scientist's lab is outside; the religious person's lab is his own being – his own body, his own soul, his own mind. The scientist has to concentrate on the object on which he is experimenting, his work has to be done with open eyes. The work of religion has to be done with closed eyes; one has to concentrate upon oneself.

And the complexity is great because in the world of religion the experimenter and the experimented upon are the same. Hence the complexity; hence the strangeness; hence the incomprehensibility; hence the illogicality. The knower and the known are the same in the world of religion. In the world of science, the knower and the known are separate; things are clearcut, demarcated. But in religion, everything merges, melts into everything else – even the knower cannot remain separate. Religion does not give you knowledge, separate from the knower; it gives you experience, not separate from the knower, but as the very essence of the knower.

To be a religious seeker one has to drop all philosophizing. One has to drop all a priori knowledge because all a priori knowledge is a hindrance; it stops your inquiry. Inquiry becomes dishonest – it becomes poisoned from the very beginning. How can you inquire if you have already concluded? To be a Christian and to be religious is impossible, to be a Hindu and to be religious is impossible. How can you be religious if you are a Hindu? Being a Hindu means that you have already concluded, you have decided what truth is. Now, what is the point of inquiry? What are you going to inquire into? All that you will be doing is finding support, arguments, for what you have already concluded. And your conclusion may be wrong – nobody knows – because your conclusion is not yours, it has been handed to you by the society.

Society is very interested in giving you conclusions, it is not interested in giving you consciousness so that you can conclude on your own. Before you become conscious, before any inquiry starts, society stuffs you with all kinds of conclusions to stop the inquiry because the inquirer is dangerous to society. The non-inquirer is convenient, the non-inquirer is obedient. He simply takes the orders, the commandments, and follows them. He is conformist, he is conventional. Once you have stuffed somebody's mind with a belief, you have drugged him. Belief is a drug. He starts believing, he goes on believing. Slowly, slowly he starts thinking that his belief is his experience.

Belief is a system of hypnosis. You go on suggesting to the child, "You are a Hindu, you are a Hindu," you take him to the temple, you lead him through religious – so-called religious – rituals, ceremonies, and by and by he becomes conditioned to the idea that he is a Hindu, that all that is Hindu is right and all that is non-Hindu is wrong.

And the same is being done in every kind of society. You have drugged the child. His very source of consciousness has been poisoned. And if you believe something, it starts appearing to be true. If you start believing something, you will find all kinds of support for it, all kinds of arguments to help it. Your ego becomes involved. It is not only a question of truth, deep down it is the question, "Who is right? Me, or you? How can I be wrong? – I have to be right." So you choose all that supports you. Life is so complex, you can find all kinds of things in life – whatsoever you choose, whatsoever you decide. If you are a pessimist, you will find all kinds of arguments in life that support pessimism. If you are an optimist, there are all kinds of arguments available to you.

The man who believes is a closed man. His windows and doors are closed; he lives in a kind of prison. He has to live in a kind of prison – if he opens the windows and doors, and the sun comes in and the wind comes in and the rain comes in, it is possible that his belief systems may be disturbed. If the truth enters from every side, it will be impossible for him to protect his beliefs. He has to hide from truth, he has to live in an enclosed world, windowless, so nothing can disturb him, so he can go on believing undisturbed. This is good for the society, but very hazardous for the health of the individual.

—

It is strange that logical scientists go on denying that there is anything inner in man. They accept the outer and they deny the inner; they accept the things in their house and they deny themselves. It is simply ludicrous, but it cannot go on for long. More and more intelligent people are searching inward because the outer search has led to death – to ultimate death.

The inner search will lead you to deeper layers of life and finally to the eternal life, in the same way as the outer search has led you to death because objects are dead. Studying dead objects and denying the living subject who is studying them... Do you think one object can study another object? – that is impossible. Can one stone observe another? Can it research the other stone?

To inquire into the objective world you need an inner consciousness, a subjectivity. That subjectivity is your consciousness. If objective science has come to nuclear weapons, ready to destroy the whole of life on the earth and turn it into pure objectivity without any subject, just the opposite happens when you reach your innermost being: everything becomes alive, conscious. The whole of existence becomes a dancing, singing, rejoicing universe, and your vision has no limits; you can see things which are not possible with objective eyes.

I had to state this just to emphasize the fact that to destroy life on the earth is going to be the greatest loss to existence, because nowhere else has it evolved to the point where a Zorba can become a Buddha. Nowhere else has it blossomed into the ultimate potential, transforming it into an actuality.

Meditation and techniques

All techniques can be helpful but they are not exactly meditation, they are just a groping in the dark. Suddenly one day, doing something, you will become a witness. Doing a meditation like Dynamic, or Kundalini or Whirling, suddenly one day the meditation will go on but you will not be identified. You will sit silently behind, you will watch it – that day, meditation will have happened; that day, technique is no longer a hindrance, no longer a help. You can enjoy it if you like, like an exercise; it gives a certain vitality, but now there is no need – now the real meditation has happened.

Meditation is witnessing. To meditate means to become a witness. Meditation is not a technique at all. This will be very confusing to you because I go on giving you techniques. In the ultimate sense, meditation is not a technique; meditation is an understanding, awareness. But you need techniques because that final understanding is very far away from you; hidden deep inside you but still very far away from you. Right this moment you can attain it. But you will not attain it because your mind goes on. This very moment it is possible, and yet impossible. Techniques will bridge the gap; they are just to bridge the gap.

So in the beginning, techniques are meditations; in the end, you will laugh – techniques are not meditation. Meditation is a totally different quality of being, it has nothing to do with anything. But it will happen only in the end; don't think it has happened in the beginning, otherwise the gap will not be bridged.

Effort

Meditation techniques are doings, because you are advised to do something – even to meditate is to do something; even to sit silently is to do something, even to not do anything is a sort of doing. So in a superficial way, all meditation techniques are doings. But in a deeper way they are not because if you succeed in them, the doing disappears.

Only in the beginning does it appear like an effort. If you succeed in it, the effort disappears and the whole thing becomes spontaneous and effortless. If you succeed in it, it is not a doing. Then no effort is needed on your part: it becomes just like breathing, it is there. But in the beginning, there is bound to be effort because the mind cannot do anything which is not an effort. If you tell it to be effortless, the whole thing seems absurd.

In the beginning, there will be effort, there will be doing – but only in the beginning, as a necessary evil. You have to remember constantly that you have to go beyond it. A moment must come when you are not doing anything about meditation; just being there and it happens. Just sitting or standing and it happens. Not doing anything, just being aware, it happens.

All these techniques are just to help you to come to an effortless moment. The inner transformation, the inner realization, cannot happen through effort because effort is a sort of tension. With effort you cannot just relax totally; the effort will become a barrier. With this background in mind, if you make effort, by and by you will become capable of leaving it also.

Simplicity

These methods which we will be discussing have been given by someone who has achieved. Remember this. They will look too simple, and they are. To our minds, things which are so simple cannot be appealing. If techniques are so simple and the abode is so near, if you are already in it, if techniques are so simple and the home is so near, you will look ridiculous to yourself – then why are you missing it? Rather than feel the ridiculousness of your own ego, you will think that such simple methods cannot help.

That is a deception. Your mind will tell you that these simple methods cannot be of any help – that they are so simple they cannot achieve anything: "To achieve divine existence, to achieve the absolute and the ultimate, how can such simple methods be used? How can they be of any help?" Your ego will say that they cannot be of any help.

Remember another thing – the ego is always interested in something which is difficult because when something is difficult, there is a challenge. If you can overcome the difficulty, your ego will feel fulfilled. The ego is never attracted toward anything that is simple – never! If you want to give your ego a challenge, something difficult must be devised. If something is simple, there is no appeal because even if you can conquer it, there will be no fulfillment of the ego. In the first place, there was nothing to be conquered: the thing was so simple. The ego asks for difficulties – hurdles to be crossed, peaks to be conquered. And the more difficult the peak, the more at ease your ego will feel.

Because these techniques are so simple, they will not have any appeal to your mind. Remember, that which appeals to the ego cannot help your spiritual growth. Only that which has no appeal to your ego can be a help toward transformation.

These techniques are so simple that you can achieve all that is possible to human consciousness, at any moment that you decide to achieve it.

Understand the technique

Mind is just a word. You don't know the complexity of it. The mind is the most complex thing in existence; there is nothing comparable to it. And it is the most delicate; you can destroy it, you can do something which then cannot be undone. These techniques are based on a very deep knowledge, on a very deep encounter with the human mind. Each technique is based on long experimentation.

So remember this: don't do anything on your own, and don't mix two techniques because their functioning is different, their ways are different, their bases are different. They lead to the same end, but as a means they are totally different. Sometimes they may even be diametrically opposite. So don't mix two techniques. Really, don't mix anything; use the technique as it is given.

Don't change it, don't improve it – you cannot improve it, and any change you bring to it will be fatal.

Before you start doing a technique, be fully alert that you have understood it. If you feel confused and you don't really know what the technique is, it is better not to do it because each technique is to bring about a revolution in you.

The right method will click

Really, when you try the right method, it clicks immediately. So I will go on talking about methods here every day. Try. Just play with them: go home and try. The right method, whenever you happen upon it, just clicks. Something explodes in you and you know "This is the right method for me." But effort is needed; and you may be surprised that suddenly one day, a method has gripped you.

Go on playing with the methods. I say playing because you should not be too serious. Just play! Something may fit you. If it fits you, then be serious and go deeply into it – intensely, honestly, with all your energy, with all your mind. But before that, just play.

I have found that while you are playing, your mind is more open. When you are serious, your mind is not so open; it is closed. So just play. Don't be too serious, just play. And these methods are simple. You can play with them.

Take one method: play with it for at least three days. If it gives you a certain feeling of affinity, if it gives you a certain feeling of well-being, if it gives you a certain feeling that it is for you, then be serious about it.

When to drop the method

One has to be very alert about dropping the method. Once you attain something, immediately drop the method, otherwise your mind will start clinging to the method. It will talk very logically to you, saying, "It is the method that is important."

Buddha used to tell a story again and again: Five idiots passed through a village. Seeing them, people were surprised because they were carrying a boat on their heads. The boat was really big; it was almost crushing those five idiots, they were almost dying under the weight of it. And people asked, "What are you doing?"

They said, "We cannot leave this boat. This is the boat that helped us to come from the other shore to this shore. How can we leave it? It is because of it that we have been able to come here. Without it, we would have died on the other shore. The night was coming close, and there were wild animals on the other shore. It was as sure as anything that by the morning we would have died. We will never leave this boat; we are indebted forever. We will carry it on our heads in sheer gratitude."

This can happen because all minds are idiots. The mind as such is idiotic.

My approach is: use the boat, use beautiful boats, use as many boats as possible, with the awareness that when the shore is reached, the boat is abandoned with no clinging. While you are in the boat, enjoy it, be thankful to it. When you get out of the boat, say thank you and move on.

If you drop the remedy, automatically you will start settling in your being. The mind clings; it never allows you to settle in your being. It keeps you interested in something that you are not: the boat.

When you don't cling to anything, there is nowhere to go – all boats have been abandoned, you cannot go anywhere; all paths have been dropped, you cannot go anywhere; all dreams and desires have disappeared, there is no way to move. Relaxation happens of its own accord. Just think of the word *relax*. Be, settle, you have come home.

More than science

Meditation is such a mystery that it can be called a science, an art, a knack, without any contradiction.

From one point of view, it is a science because there is a clear-cut technique that has to be done. There are no exceptions to it, it is almost like a scientific law.

But from a different point of view, it can also be said to be an art. Science is an extension of the mind – it is mathematics, it is logic, it is rational. Meditation belongs to the heart, not to the mind – it is not logic, it is closer to love. It is not like other scientific activities, but is more like music, poetry, painting, dancing; hence, it can be called an art.

But meditation is such a great mystery that calling it a science and an art does not exhaust it. It is a knack – either you get it or you don't get it.

Slowly, slowly more and more moments will be coming. As you become skillful, as you learn the knack of not getting involved in the mind, as you learn the art of remaining aloof, away from the mind, as you learn the science of creating a distance between you and your own thoughts, more and more meditation will be showering on you. The more it showers, the more it transforms you.

A day comes, a day of great blessings, when meditation becomes your natural state.

5

TIPS FOR MEDITATORS

Preparation: space, place, posture, comfort

When you are trying to meditate, put the phone off the hook, disengage yourself. Put a notice on the door that for one hour nobody should knock, that you are meditating. When you go into the meditation room, take your shoes off because you are walking on sacred ground. And not only take your shoes off, but everything that you are preoccupied with. Consciously leave everything with the shoes. Go inside unoccupied.

Find a place where nature has not yet been disturbed, polluted. If you cannot find such a place, then just close your door and sit in your own room. If it is possible, have a special room for meditation in your house. Just a small corner will do, but especially for meditation. Why especially for meditation? – because each kind of act creates its own vibration. If you simply meditate in that place, that place becomes meditative.

Every day you meditate, it absorbs your vibration when you are in meditation. And the next day when you come, those vibrations start falling back on you. They help, they reciprocate, they respond.

When a person has really become a meditator, he can meditate sitting before a cinema screen, he can meditate on a railway platform.

For fifteen years, I was continually traveling around the country, continually traveling – day in, day out, day in, day out, year in, year out – always on a train, on a plane, in a car. That makes no difference. Once you have become really rooted in your being, nothing makes any difference. But this is not for the beginner.

Your posture should be such that you can forget your body. What is comfort? – when you forget your body, you are comfortable. When you are reminded continuously of the body, you are uncomfortable. So whether you sit in a chair or you sit on the ground is not the point. Be comfortable because if you are not comfortable in the body, you cannot long for other blessings which belong to deeper layers: the first layer missed, all other layers are closed. If you really want to be happy, blissful, then start from the very beginning to be blissful. Comfort of the body is a basic need for anybody who is trying to reach inner ecstasies.

Movement and cleansing

I never tell people to begin with just sitting. Begin from where beginning is easy. Otherwise, you will start to feel many things unnecessarily – things that are not there.

If you begin with sitting, you will feel much disturbance inside. The more you try to just sit, the more disturbance will be felt. You will become aware only of your insane mind and nothing else. It will create depression and you will feel frustrated, you will not feel blissful. Rather, you will begin to feel that you are insane. And sometimes you may really go insane!

If you make a sincere effort to "just sit," you may really go insane. Only because people do not really try sincerely does insanity not happen more often. With a sitting posture, you begin to know so much madness inside you that, if you are sincere and continue it, you may really go insane. It has happened before, so many times. So I never suggest anything that can create frustration, depression, sadness – anything that will allow you to be too aware of your insanity. You may not be ready to be aware of all the insanity that is inside you.

You must be allowed to get to know certain things gradually. Knowledge is not always good. It must unfold itself slowly, as your capacity to absorb it grows. I start with your insanity, not with a sitting posture. I allow your insanity. If you dance madly, the opposite happens within you. With a mad dance, you begin to be aware of a silent point within you; with sitting silently, you begin to be aware of madness. The opposite is always the point of awareness.

With dancing madly, chaotically, with crying, with chaotic breathing, I allow your madness. Then you begin to be aware of a subtle point, a deep point inside you which is silent and still, in contrast to the madness on the periphery. You will feel very blissful: at your center there is an inner silence. But if you are just sitting, then the inner one is the mad one. You are silent on the outside, but inside you are mad.

If you begin with something active – something positive, alive, moving – it will be better. Then you will begin to feel an inner stillness growing. The more it grows, the more it will be possible for you to use a sitting posture or a lying posture, and the more silent meditation will be possible. But by then, things will be different, totally different.

A meditation technique that begins with movement, action, helps you in other ways also. It becomes a catharsis. When you are just sitting, you are frustrated: your mind wants to move and you are just sitting. Every muscle turns, every nerve turns. You are trying to force something upon yourself that is not natural for you. You have divided yourself into the one who is forcing and the one who is being forced. And really, the part that is being forced and suppressed is the more authentic part; it is a more major part of your mind than the part that is suppressing, and the major part is bound to win.

That which you are suppressing is to be thrown out, not suppressed. It has become an accumulation within you because you have been constantly suppressing it. The whole upbringing, the civilization, education, is suppressive. You have been suppressing much that could have been thrown out very easily with a different education, with a more conscious education, with a more aware parenthood. With a better awareness of the inner mechanism of the mind, the culture could have allowed you to throw out many things.

For example, when a child is angry we tell him, "Do not be angry." He begins to suppress anger. By and by, what was a momentary happening becomes permanent. Now he will not act angry, but he will remain angry. We have accumulated so much anger from what were just momentary things. No one can be angry continuously unless anger has been suppressed. Anger is a momentary thing that comes and goes; if it is expressed, you are no longer angry. So as far as I am concerned, I would allow the child to be angry more authentically. Be angry, but be deeply in it. Do not suppress it.

Of course, there will be problems. If we say, "Be angry," then you are going to be angry at someone. But a child can be molded. He can be given a pillow and told, "Be angry with the pillow. Be violent with the pillow." From the very beginning, a child can be brought up in a way in which the anger is deviated. Some object can be given to him and he can go on throwing the object until his anger goes. Within minutes, within seconds, he will have dissipated his anger and there will be no accumulation of it.

You have accumulated anger, sex, violence, greed – everything. Now this accumulation is a madness within you. It is there, inside you. If you begin with any suppressive meditation – for example, with just sitting – you are suppressing all of this, you are not allowing it to be released. So I begin with a catharsis. First, let the suppressions be thrown into the air. And when you can throw your anger into the air, you have become mature.

Three essentials

Meditation has a few essential things in it, whatever the method, and those few essentials are necessary in every method. The first is a relaxed state: no fight with the mind, no control of the mind, no concentration. Second, just watching with a relaxed awareness whatever is going on, without any interference – just watching the mind, silently, without any judgment, evaluation.

The three things are: relaxation, watching, no judgment, and slowly, slowly a great silence descends over you. All movement within you ceases. You are, but there is no sense of "I am" – just a pure space. There are one hundred and twelve methods of meditation. I have talked on all those methods. They differ in their constitution, but the fundamentals remain the same: relaxation, watchfulness, a nonjudgmental attitude.

Playfulness

Millions of people miss meditation because meditation has taken on a wrong connotation. It looks very serious, looks gloomy, has something of the church in it. It looks as if it is only for people who are either dead, or almost dead, who are gloomy, serious, have long faces; who have lost festivity, fun, playfulness, celebration. And these are the qualities of meditation. A really meditative person is playful, life is fun for him. Life is a *leela*, a play. He enjoys it tremendously. He is not serious, he is relaxed.

Patience

Don't be in a hurry. So often hurrying causes delay. As you thirst, wait patiently – the deeper the waiting, the sooner it comes.

You have sown the seed, now sit in the shade and watch what

happens. The seed will break, it will blossom, but you cannot speed up the process. Doesn't everything need time? Work you must, but leave the results to existence. Nothing in life is ever wasted, especially steps taken toward truth.

But at times impatience comes; impatience comes with thirst, but this is an obstacle. Keep the thirst and throw out the impatience.

Do not confuse impatience with thirst. With thirst there is yearning, but no struggle; with impatience there is struggle, but no yearning. With longing there is waiting, but no demanding; with impatience there is demanding, but no waiting. With thirst there are silent tears; with impatience there is restless struggle.

Truth cannot be attained by aggression; it is attained through surrender, not through struggle. It is conquered through total surrender.

Be without goals

Meditation is not a serious phenomenon. It is a song, a dance, a celebration. Don't take meditation religiously, take it playfully. To take it religiously is to miss the whole point. It is religion, but don't take it religiously. It has to be taken as fun, just like children making sand castles, with no particular goal in view, just enjoying the very activity itself.

Meditation is not a means to any end, but an end unto itself. Love it, enjoy it, and don't ask for any results. Results come but don't ask for them, then they come sooner. Tremendous consequences are there, consequences that will transform your whole life, but you need not bother about them.

Meditation should not be done with any motive. In life there must be a few things which you do without any motive – unless your life is just a marketplace and then everything is a commodity. Meditation is not a commodity.

Do not look for results in meditation – this is an obstruction. Do not seek to repeat any meditative experience, for this too is a hindrance.

When meditating, just meditate, the rest then happens by itself.

Enjoy

While aware, enjoy awareness and while unaware, enjoy un-awareness – nothing is wrong because unawareness is like a rest. Otherwise, awareness will become a tension. If you are awake twenty-four hours a day, how many days do you think you can stay alive? Without food, a man can live for three months; without sleep, within three weeks he will go mad and will try to commit suicide. In the day you are alert; in the night you relax, and that relaxation helps you to be more alert, fresh again in the day. The energies have passed through a rest period; they are more alive again in the morning.

The same will happen in meditation: for a few moments you are perfectly aware, at the peak; a few moments you are in the valley, resting – awareness has disappeared, you have forgotten about it. But what is wrong in this? It is simple. Through unawareness, awareness will arise again – fresh, young, and this will go on.

If you can enjoy both, you become the third, and that is the point to be understood. If you can enjoy both, it means you are neither – neither awareness nor unawareness – you are the one who enjoys both. Something of the beyond enters. In fact, this is the real witness.

6

OBSTACLES TO MEDITATION

The ego

You are continuously prepared by the society, by the family, by the school, by the church, by everybody around you, to be egoistic. Even modern psychology is based on strengthening the ego. The whole idea of modern psychology, modern education, is that unless a person has a very strong ego, he will not be able to struggle in life. And in life there is so much competition that, if you are a humble man, everybody will push you aside; you will always remain at the back. You need a very steely, strong ego to fight in this competitive world; only then can you become a success in any field. It may be business, it may be politics – it can be any profession – you need a very assertive personality, and our whole society is geared to produce an assertive personality in the child.

From the very beginning we start telling him, "Come first in your class" and when he does, everybody praises him. What are you doing? You are feeding his ego from the very beginning. You are giving him a certain ambition: "You can become the president of the country; you can become the prime minister." He starts the journey with these ideas, and his ego goes on becoming bigger and bigger as he succeeds.

In every way the ego is the greatest disease that can happen to man. If you succeed, your ego becomes big – that is a danger because then you will have to remove a big rock which is blocking the path. Or, if the ego is small, you have not been successful, you have proved to be a failure, then your ego will become a wound. Then it hurts, then it creates an inferiority complex – then too it creates a problem. Then you are always afraid to enter anything, even meditation, because you know you are a failure, you know that you are going to fail – that has become your mind because you have failed everywhere. And meditation is such a great thing, so you cannot succeed.

If you enter meditation with this idea – that you are bound to fail, that it is your destiny, that it is your fate – then of course you cannot succeed. So, if the ego is big it prevents you. And if the ego is very small, it becomes a wound, then it prevents you. In each case the ego is one of the problems.

Your real center is not only your center, it is the center of the whole. But we have created small centers of our own, home-made, manufactured by ourselves. There is a need for this because the child is born without any boundary, with no idea of who he is. It is a survival necessity. How will he survive? He has to be given a name, he has to be given an idea of who he is. Of course this idea comes from the outside: somebody says you are beautiful, somebody says you are intelligent, some-body says you are so alive. You gather the things that people say. Out of all that people say about you, you gather a certain image. You never look into yourself, at who you are.

This image is going to be false because nobody else can know who you are, and nobody else can say who you are. Your inner reality is not available to anybody except you. Your inner reality is impenetrable to anybody except you. Only you can be there.

The day you realize that your identity is false, put together, that you have collected opinions from people... Sometime just think, just sit silently and think who you are. Many ideas will arise. Just go on watching from where they come and you will be able to find the source. Something comes from your mother – much; about eighty to ninety percent. Something comes from your father, something comes from your schoolteachers, some-thing comes from your friends, something from the society. Just watch: you will be able to tell from where each idea comes. Nothing comes from you, not even one percent comes from you. What type of identity is this, in which you have not contributed at all? And you are the only one who could have contributed, in fact the whole hundred percent.

There are things which nobody can do for you. At least one thing can never be done by anybody else – that is, to give you the answer to who you are. No, you have to go on; you have to dig deep into your own being. Layers and layers of identity, false identity, have to be broken.

There is fear when one enters oneself because chaos comes in. Somehow you have managed with your false identity. You have settled with it. You know your name is this or that; you have certain credentials, certificates, degrees, universities, colleges, prestige, money, heritage. You have certain ways to define your-self. You have a certain definition, howsoever workable – but it works. Going in means dropping this workable definition. There will be chaos.

Before you can come to your center, you will have to pass through a very chaotic state. That's why there is fear. Nobody wants to go in. People go on teaching "Know thyself"; we hear it, but we never listen. We never bother about it. There is a very certain idea in the mind that chaos will be let loose and you will be lost in it, you will be engulfed in it. Because of the fear of that chaos, we go on clinging to anything from the outside. But this is wasting your life.

The mind and its tricks

The second hindrance on the path of meditation is your constantly chattering mind. You cannot sit even for a single minute; the mind goes on chattering: relevant, irrelevant, meaningful, meaningless... Thoughts go on. It is a constant traffic and it is always rush hour.

—

You see a flower and you verbalize it; you see a man passing and you verbalize it. Every situation is verbalized. The mind has become just a verbalizing mechanism. It can translate every existential thing into a word – everything is being transformed constantly into words. These words create a barrier, these words become an imprisonment. These words – this constant flow, transformation of things into words, of existence into words – are the barrier, are the obstacle toward the meditative mind.

So the first requirement toward meditative growth is to be aware of this constant verbalizing and to be able to stop it. Just see things; don't verbalize. Be aware of their presence but don't change them into words. Live with things without language; with people without language; with situations without language. This is not impossible. This is natural and possible.

—

In meditation, sometimes you feel a sort of emptiness that is not really emptiness. I call it just "a sort of emptiness." When you are meditating, for certain moments, for a few seconds, you will feel as if the thought process has stopped. In the beginning these gaps will come. But because you are feeling as if the thought process has stopped, this is again a thought process, a very subtle thought process. What are you doing? You are saying inside, "The thought process has stopped." But what is this? This is a second thought process which has started. And you say, "This is emptiness." You say, "Now something is going to happen." What is this? Again a new thought process has started.

When this happens again, don't become a victim of it. When you feel a certain silence is descending, don't start verbalizing it because you are destroying it. Wait – not for something – simply wait. Don't do anything. Don't say, "This is emptiness." The moment you have said that, you have destroyed it. Just look at it, penetrate it, encounter it – but wait, don't verbalize it. What is the hurry? Through verbalization the mind has again entered from a different route, and you are deceived. Be alert about this trick of the mind.

In the beginning it is bound to happen, so whenever it happens, just wait. Don't fall in the trap. Don't say anything, remain silent. Then you will enter emptiness, and then it will not be temporary because once you have known the real emptiness, you cannot lose it. The real cannot be lost; that is its quality.

There are patterns the seeker gets entangled with. The first thing is: most seekers are lost in an illusory feeling that they have arrived. It is like the kind of dream in which you feel you are awake. You are still dreaming – your feeling of being awake is part of the dream. The same kind of thing happens to the seeker. The mind is capable of creating the illusion: "Now there is nowhere to go, you have arrived."

In the ancient scriptures of the East, it is called the power of maya. Mind has the hypnotic power to create any illusion. And if you are after a certain thing, desperately, it is one of the functions of the mind to create the illusion to stop your desperateness. It happens every day to everybody in dreams, but people don't learn...

If at night you go to bed hungry, that night you are going to dream about eating delicious food. The mind is trying to help you so that your sleep is not disturbed; otherwise you are hungry and you are bound to be awakened by your hunger. The mind gives you a dream that you are eating delicious food of your choice, which satisfies your mind. The hunger remains but sleep is not disturbed. The hunger is covered by the illusion of the dream; it protects your sleep.

This is the ordinary function of the mind; and on a higher plane, the same thing happens. One is an ordinary sleep and an ordinary awakening that mind prevents. On the path, it is an extraordinary sleep and an extraordinary awakening, but the mind is programmed – it is just a mechanical thing. It simply does its work without bothering, because it has no way of checking whether it is ordinary sleep or spiritual sleep, ordinary awakening or spiritual awakening.

To the mind it is all the same. Its function is to keep your sleep intact and create a barrier for anything that disturbs your sleep. If you are hungry, it gives you food; if you are desperately in search of truth, it gives you truth, it gives you enlightenment. Ask for anything, and it is ready to give it to you. It can create the illusion of the real thing – that is its intrinsic power.

—

Everything that you can watch is part of the mind – that's the very key to unlock the door. Everything that can be watched – kundalini arising, lotuses opening, beautiful fragrances and light inside... All can be watched, so that simply means they are subtle processes of thought. Mind is playing, trying to play its last tricks, trying to enchant you: "Look, what are you doing? Trying to drop me? I can supply such a good circus and I contain so many mysteries. What are you doing? Trying to go beyond me? Then watch this light, watch this energy, and see: your third eye is opening." These are all tricks of the mind, subtle tricks. One has to remain absolutely unaffected.

Those are the real temptations. There is no Devil other than the mind. If one can go on watching and enjoying these temptations: "Yes, you go on playing your tricks – I am ready to watch, I will watch everything. I will watch even nothing..." That is the final and ultimate strategy. The mind says "Okay, you are interested in nothing? Have it!" If you cling to nothing you are back in the mind; the mind has conquered you, you have been defeated.

So you say "Okay, I will even watch nothing. I am not going

to be entangled in anything again, even nothing." And then the real nothing happens; it is no longer a thought. You don't see it, you can't hold it, you can't touch it. All has disappeared; even the idea of nothing is no longer there. You are not feeling a great joy, "Look, now I have achieved nothing. That's what happens when a man becomes a buddha." Even that is not there; hence Buddha says "If you meet me on the way, kill me immediately." That's what he means: even if you come to the idea "Now I have become the Buddha," kill it immediately. That is the last temptation of the mind.

Go on watching and watching and watching till there is nothing to watch, not even nothing to watch. Then the watcher is left alone, then there is no object. When subjectivity is left alone, in that absolute silence is the revolution.

Judgments

My understanding and experience of meditation is to let it be whatever it is; just remain silent, without any concern, without any judgment, without any appreciation or condemnation. Soon all the dust will settle and you will be left behind in your immense glory, in your tremendous beauty, in your peaks of consciousness.

—

Judgment comes from the past, and witnessing is a present consciousness. Witnessing is now and here, and judgment is somewhere else, in the past. Whenever you judge anything, try a small experiment: try to find out who has given you this idea. And if you go deeply into it, you will be surprised: you can even hear your mother saying it, or your father, or your teacher in school. You can hear their voices still there resounding in your memory, but it is not yours. Whatsoever is not yours is ugly; and whatsoever is yours is beautiful, it has grace.

—

Meditation is a simple method. Your mind is like a TV screen. Memories are passing, images are passing, thoughts, desires, a thousand and one things are passing; it is always rush hour. And the road is almost like an Indian road – no traffic rules, everybody is going in every direction. One has to watch it without any evaluation, without any judgment, without any choice – simply

45

watching unconcerned, as if it has nothing to do with you, you are just a witness. That is choiceless awareness.

If you choose, if you say "This thought is good – let me have it" or "It is a beautiful desire, a beautiful dream, I should enjoy it a little more, I can go into it a little deeper"... If you choose, you lose your witnessing. If you say "This is bad, this is immoral, this is a sin, I should throw it out," you start struggling and again you lose your witnessing.

You can lose your witnessing in two ways; either being for or against. And the whole secret of meditation is to be neither for nor against, but unconcerned, cool, without any preference, likes, dislikes, without any choice. If you can manage even a few moments of that witnessing, you will be surprised how much bliss happens, how ecstatic one becomes.

—

The flow of thoughts moves in the mind, just watch the thoughts. Don't judge what is good, what is bad. Let them pass by, just as the traffic passes by. You are standing at the side of the road just looking: good people are going by, bad people are going by, dishonest people are going by, honest people too – moral, immoral – what's it to you? You are standing at the side of the road, just watching. You are only a watcher, merely a witness. And you will be amazed, if you stand at the side of the stream of thoughts... Thinking is just a flow. You are separate from it. You are not the thoughts, you are the one who sees the thoughts. You just have to awaken and remember: "I am the watcher."

Let the thoughts go on moving and now if "Rama, Rama" comes along, or "Coca-Cola" comes along, whatever comes along, just let them go on passing by. Standing at a distance, just go on watching peacefully. You are neither for nor against. Don't say, "Aha! A good thought has come." If you say this, you are caught. You will grab hold of the thought you think is good and you will create an attachment to it. You will want it to come again and again. You will make friends with it, you will be married to it. Or a thought will come and you will say, "This is bad, I don't want to see it," and turn your head aside. This too will follow you because it will be angry as you have insulted it. You have denied it, negated it. It will knock on the door again and again. It will say, "Look at me!"

Whatever you deny returns again and again. Try observing this. Deny any thought and observe – it will come again and again, it will torture you around the clock. If you hold onto anything you are caught; renounce it, and you are also caught. Indulgence catches you and renunciation also catches you. There is freedom only in the witness – not in indulgence, not in renunciation. Don't say "Very beautiful," and don't say "Very bad." Don't say anything – there is no need to say anything – just observe. Can't you merely watch as a mirror watches? Even if a beautiful woman comes in front of a mirror, the mirror doesn't say, "Wait a bit, stay a little longer." Nor does it strike up a conversation. If an ugly woman comes along, it doesn't say, "Walk quickly by, move along, get lost, go and torture some other mirror."

A mirror just watches. In the same way, when you become a witness like a mirror, all your thoughts start to become quiet on their own. A moment will come when the pathway of thoughts becomes deserted, no one comes. In that silence, the voice of existence is heard for the first time.

7

QUESTIONS ABOUT MEDITATION

Osho,
You continually encourage us to be aware, to be a witness.
But is the witness only a spectator? Can a witnessing
consciousness really sing, dance and taste life?

Mind is bound to raise this question sooner or later, because mind is very much afraid of your becoming a witness. Why is the mind so afraid of it? – because your becoming a witness is the death of the mind.

Mind is a doer, it wants to do things, and witnessing is a state of non-doing. The mind is afraid: "If you become a witness, I will not be needed anymore." And, in a way, the mind is right.

Once the witness arises in you, the mind has to disappear, just as if you bring light into your room and the darkness has to disappear – it is inevitable. Mind can exist only if you remain fast asleep, because mind is a state of dreaming and dreams can exist only in sleep.

By becoming a witness you are no longer asleep, you are awake. You become awareness – so crystal clear, so young and fresh, so vital and potent. You become a flame – intense, burning from both ends – as if, in that state of intensity, light, consciousness, mind dies, mind commits suicide. Hence the mind is afraid.

And the mind will create many problems for you, it will raise many, many questions. It will make you hesitate to take the jump into the unknown, it will try to pull you back. It will try to convince you: "With me is safety, security; with me you are living under a shelter, well-guarded. I take every care of you. With me you are efficient, skillful. The moment you leave me, you will have to leave all your knowledge and you will have to leave all your securities, safeties. You will have to drop your armor and you will be going into the unknown. You are unnecessarily taking a risk for no reason at all." It will try to bring beautiful rationalizations. This is one of the rationalizations which almost always happens to every meditator.

It is not you who is asking the question; it is the mind, your enemy, who is putting the questions through you. It is the mind who is saying, "Osho, you continuously tell us to be aware, to be a witness. But can a witnessing consciousness really sing, dance and taste life?" Yes – in fact only a witnessing consciousness can really sing, dance and taste life. It will appear to be a paradox. It is. But all that is true is always paradoxical, remember. If truth is not paradoxical, it is not truth at all; then it is something else.

Paradox is a basic, intrinsic quality of truth – let this sink into your heart forever. Truth as such is paradoxical. Although not all paradoxes are truths, all truths are paradoxes. The truth has to be a paradox because it has to be both the negative and the positive pole – and yet a transcendence. It has to be life and death, and plus. By "plus" I mean the transcendence of both – both and both not. That is the ultimate paradox.

When you are in the mind, how can you sing? The mind creates misery; out of misery there can be no song. When you are in the mind, how can you dance? Yes, you can go through certain empty gestures called dance, but it is not a real dance.

Only a Meera knows a real dance, or a Krishna, or a Chaitanya. These are the people who know real dance. Others know only the technique of dancing, but there is nothing overflowing; their energies are stagnant. People who are living in the mind are living in the ego, and the ego cannot dance. It can make a performance but not a dance.

The real dance happens only when you have become a witness. Then you are so blissful that the very bliss starts overflowing – that is the dance. The very bliss starts singing; a song arises on its own accord. And only when you are a witness can you taste life.

I can understand your question. You are worried that by becoming a witness one will become merely a spectator of life. No, to be a spectator is one thing, and to be a witness a totally different thing, qualitatively different.

A spectator is indifferent, he is dull, he is in a kind of sleep. He does not participate in life. He is afraid, he is a coward. He stands by the side of the road and simply goes on seeing others living. That's what you are doing all your life: somebody else acts in a movie and you watch it. You are a spectator. People are glued to their chairs for hours together before their TVs – spectators. Somebody else is singing; you are listening. Somebody else is dancing, you are just a spectator. Somebody else is loving and you are just seeing it. You are not a participant. Professionals are doing what you should have done on your own. A witness is not a spectator. Then what is a witness? A witness is one who participates yet remains alert. A witness is in a state of *wu-wei*. That is Lao Tzu's word: it means action through inaction. A witness is not one who has escaped from life. He lives in life, lives far more totally, far more passionately, and yet remains deep down a watcher; goes on remembering "I am a consciousness."

Try it walking on the road: remember that you are a consciousness. Walking continues – and something new is added, a new richness, a new beauty. Something interior is added to the outward act. You become a flame of consciousness, and then the walking has a totally different joy to it; you are on the earth and yet your feet are not touching the earth at all.

That's what Buddha has said: "Pass through a river, but don't let the water touch your feet."

Osho,
Sometimes when I meditate I become aware of a lot of
ugliness inside. How can I accept the dark side of my mind?

The basic thing to be understood is that you are not the mind – neither the bright one nor the dark one. If you get identified with the beautiful part, then it is impossible to disidentify yourself from the ugly part; they are two sides of the same coin. You can have it whole, or you can throw it away whole, but you cannot divide it.

The whole anxiety of man is that he wants to choose that which looks beautiful, bright; he wants to choose all the silver linings, leaving the dark cloud behind. But he does not know that silver linings cannot exist without the dark cloud. The dark cloud is the background, absolutely necessary for silver linings to show.

Choosing is anxiety. Choosing is creating trouble for yourself. Being choiceless means: the mind is there and it has a dark side and it has a bright side – so what? What has it to do with you? Why should you be worried about it?

The moment you are not choosing, all worry disappears. A great acceptance arises, that this is how the mind has to be, this is the nature of the mind – and it is not your problem because you are not the mind. If you *were* the mind, there would have been no problem at all. Then who would choose and who would think of transcending? And who would try to accept and understand acceptance?

You are separate, totally separate. You are only a witness and nothing else.

An observer who gets identified with anything that he finds pleasant and forgets that the unpleasant is coming just behind it as a shadow... You are not troubled by the pleasant side – you rejoice in it. The trouble comes when the polar opposite asserts itself – then you are torn apart.

But you started the whole trouble. Falling from being just a witness, you became identified. The biblical story of the fall is just a fiction. But this is the real fall: the fall from being a witness into getting identified with something and losing your witnessing.

Just try once in a while to let the mind be whatever it is. Remember, you are not it. And you are going to have a great surprise. The less identified you are, the less powerful the mind becomes because its power comes from your identification; it sucks your blood. But when you start to stand aloof and away, the mind starts shrinking.

The day you are completely unidentified with the mind, even for a single moment, there is the revelation. Mind simply dies; it is no longer there. Where it was so full, where it was so continuous – day in, day out, waking, sleeping, it was there – suddenly it is not there. You look all around and it is emptiness, it is nothingness.

With the mind, the self disappears. Then there is only a certain quality of awareness, with no I in it. At the most you can call it something similar to am-ness, but not I-ness. To be even more exact, it is is-ness because even in am-ness some shadow of the I is still there. The moment you know its is-ness, it has become universal.

With the disappearance of the mind the self disappears. So many things disappear which were so important to you, so troublesome to you. You were trying to solve them and they were becoming more and more complicated; everything was a problem, an anxiety, and there seemed to be no way out.

Mind is just a procession of thoughts passing in front of you on the screen of the brain. You are an observer. But you start getting identified with beautiful things – those are bribes. And once you get caught in the beautiful things, you are also caught in the ugly things because mind cannot exist without duality.

Awareness cannot exist *with* duality, and mind cannot exist without duality. Awareness is non-dual, and mind is dual. So just watch. I don't teach you any solutions. I teach you *the* solution: just get back a little and watch. Create a distance between you and your mind.

Whether it is good – beautiful, delicious, something that you would like to enjoy closely – or it is ugly, remain as far away as possible. Look at it just the way you look at a film. But people get identified even with films.

I have not seen a movie for a long time. When I was young, I have seen people weeping, tears falling – and nothing is happening! It is good that in a movie theater it is dark; it saves them from feeling embarrassed: nothing is happening!

I used to ask my father, "Did you see? The fellow by your side was crying!"

He said, "The whole hall was crying. The scene was such…"

"But," I said, "there is only a screen and nothing else. Nobody is killed, there is no tragedy happening – just the projection of a film, just pictures moving on a screen. People laugh, and they weep, and for three hours they are almost lost. They become part of the movie, they become identified with some character."

My father said to me, "If you are raising questions about people's reactions, then you cannot enjoy the film."

I said, "I can enjoy the film, but I don't want to cry; I don't see any enjoyment in it. I can see it as a film, but I don't want to become a part of it. These people are all becoming a part of it."

You get identified with anything. People get identified with other people and then they create misery for themselves. They get identified with things, then they get miserable if that thing is missing.

Identification is the root cause of your misery. And each identification is identification with the mind. Just step aside, let the mind pass. And soon you will be able to see that there is no problem at all.

Osho,
Sometimes I feel physical pain during meditation. What
should I do?

If you feel pain, be attentive to it; don't do anything. Attention is the great sword – it cuts everything. Simply pay attention to the pain.

For example, you are sitting silently in the last part of a meditation, unmoving, and you feel many problems in the body. You feel the leg is going dead, there is itching in the hand, you feel ants are creeping on the body and you have looked many times – there are no ants. The creeping is inside, not outside. What should you do? You feel the leg is going dead – be watchful, just pay total attention to it. You feel itching – don't scratch, that will not help. Just pay attention. Don't even open your eyes. Just pay attention inwardly and just wait and watch; within seconds the itching will disappear.

Whatsoever happens – even if you feel pain, severe pain in the stomach or in the head... It is possible because in meditation the whole body changes. It changes its chemistry. New things start happening; the body is in a chaos. Sometimes the stomach will be affected because you have suppressed many emotions there and they are all stirred. Sometimes you will feel like vomiting, nausea. Sometimes you will feel a severe pain in the head because the meditation is changing the inner structure of your brain. You are really in a chaos passing through meditation. Soon things will settle. But, for the time being, everything will be unsettled.

So what are you to do? Simply see the pain in the head; watch it. Be a watcher. Just forget that you are a doer, and by and by everything subsides and subsides so beautifully and so gracefully that you cannot believe it unless you know it. It is not just that the pain disappears from the head: if the energy which was creating pain is watched, the pain disappears and the same energy becomes pleasure. The energy is the same. Pain and pleasure are two dimensions of the same energy.

Osho,
When I meditate, my mind still goes 500 miles an hour. Am
I wasting my time?

Your mind is mighty slow. Only 500 miles per hour? Do you think this is fast? You are mighty slow. Mind knows no speed; it goes so fast, it is faster than light. Light travels 186,000 miles in a second, mind is faster than that. But nothing to be worried about – that is the beauty of the mind, that is a great quality. Rather than taking it negatively, rather than fighting with it, befriend the mind.

You say: "During the meditations my mind still goes 500 miles per hour." Let it go! Let it go faster! Be a watcher, watch the mind going around so fast, with such speed. Enjoy it, enjoy this play of the mind. In Sanskrit we have a special term for it; we call it *chidvilas*, the play of consciousness. Enjoy it, this play of mind rushing toward stars, moving so fast from here and there, jumping all over existence. What is wrong in it? Let it be a beautiful dance, accept it.

My feeling is that you are trying to stop it – you cannot do that. Nobody can stop the mind. Yes, the mind stops one day, but nobody can stop it. The mind stops, but that is not by your effort, the mind stops out of your understanding.

Just watch and try to see what is happening, why the mind is rushing; it is not rushing without a reason. You must be ambitious. Try to see why the mind is rushing, where it is rushing. You must be ambitious; if it thinks about money, then try to understand: the mind is not the question. You start dreaming about money, that you have won a lottery or this and that, and then you even start planning how to spend it, what to purchase and what not. Or the mind thinks you have become the president, the prime minister, and then you start thinking what to do now, how to run the country, or the world. Just watch the mind, what the mind is going toward. There must be a deep seed in you. You cannot stop the mind unless that seed disappears.

The mind is simply following the order of your innermost

seed. Somebody is thinking about sex, then somewhere there is repressed sexuality. Watch where the mind is rushing to, look deep into yourself and find where the seeds are.

I have heard: A parson was very worried. "Listen," he said to his verger, "somebody has stolen my bicycle."

"Where have you been on it, rector?" inquired that verger.

"Only round the parish on my calls."

The verger suggested that the best plan would be for the rector to direct his Sunday sermon to the Ten Commandments. "When you get to 'Thou shalt not steal,' you and I will watch the faces – we will soon see."

Sunday came. The rector started in fine flow about the commandments, then lost his thread, changed his subject, and trailed off lamely.

"Sir," said the verger, "I thought you were going to…"

"I know, Giles, I know. But you see, when I got to 'Thou shalt not commit adultery,' I suddenly remembered where I had left my bicycle."

Just see where you have left your bicycle. The mind is rushing for certain reasons. The mind needs understanding, awareness; don't try to stop it. If you try to stop it, in the first place you cannot succeed; in the second place, if you can succeed – one can succeed if one makes perseverant effort for years – if you can succeed, you will become dull. No satori will happen out of it.

In the first place, you cannot succeed and it is good that you cannot succeed. If you can succeed, if you manage to succeed, that will be very unfortunate – you will become dull, you will lose intelligence. With that speed there is intelligence, with that speed there is continuous sharpening of the sword of thinking, logic, intellect. Please don't try to stop it. I am not in favor of dullards, and I am not here to help anybody to become stupid.

Many people have become stupid in the name of religion. They have become almost idiots, just trying to stop the mind without any understanding about why it is going with such speed – why, in the first place? The mind cannot go without a reason. Without going into the reason in the layers, the deep layers of the unconscious, they just try to stop it. They can stop it, but they will have to pay a price, and the price will be that their intelligence will be lost.

You can go around India and find thousands of sannyasins, mahatmas. Look into their eyes – yes, they are good people, nice but stupid. If you look in their eyes there is no intelligence, you will not see any lightning. They are uncreative people, they have not created anything; they just sit there. They are vegetating, they are not alive; they have not helped the world in any way. They have not even produced a painting or a poem or a song, because even to produce a poem you will need intelligence, you will need certain qualities of the mind.

I would not suggest that you stop the mind, rather that you understand it. With understanding, there happens a miracle. The miracle is that with understanding, by and by – when you understand the causes and those causes are looked into deeply, and through that looking deeply into those causes, those causes disappear – the mind slows down. But intelligence is not lost because the mind is not forced.

It feels like my witnessing is flashing "on again, off again"
like a car's turn signals: witnessing yes, witnessing no.
What does this mean?

You have to remember that there is something more behind these witnessing moments which is witnessing all this process. Who is witnessing that sometimes you are witnessing and sometimes you are not witnessing? Something is constant.

Your witnessing has become just an indicator; don't be bothered by it. Your emphasis should be on the eternal, the constant, the continuum – and it is there. And it is in everyone, we have just forgotten it.

But even in times when we have forgotten it, it is there in its absolute perfection. It is like a mirror which is able to mirror everything, is still mirroring everything, but you are standing with your back toward the mirror. The poor mirror is mirroring your back.

Turn, it will mirror your face. Open your heart; it will mirror your heart. Put everything on the table, don't even hide a single card and it will reflect your whole reality.

But if you go on standing with your back to the mirror looking all around the world asking people, "Who am I?" then it is up
to you, because there are idiots who will come and teach you:
"This is the way. Do this and you will know who you are." No
method is needed, just a one-hundred-and-eighty-degree turn –
and that is not a method. The mirror is your very being.

And when you say, witnessing, yes, and then it disappears
and you say no – again it appears, you say yes... It simply shows
that there is something behind all these moments of witnessing and not witnessing. The true witness, which is reflecting the
changing process of what you think is your witness, is behind all
this. This is not the true witness, it is only the indicator. Forget
the indicator.

Remember the constant mirroring that goes on twenty-four
hours within you, silently watching everything. Slowly, slowly
clean it – there is so much dust on it, centuries of dust. Remove
the dust.

And one day, when the mirror is completely clean, those
moments of witnessing and not-witnessing will disappear; you
will be simply a witness.

And unless you find that eternity of witnessing, all other
kinds of witnessing are part of mind. They have no value.

Osho,
There are so many products available now that claim to
bring us to meditation. Can they really help?

So many machines are being developed around the world,
pretending that they can give you meditation: "You just have to
plug your ears with earphones and relax and within ten minutes
you will reach the state of meditation." This is utter stupidity.

Mind functions on one wavelength when it is awake; when
it is dreaming it functions on a different wavelength. When it
is fast asleep it functions on another wavelength. But none of
these are meditation.

For thousands of years we have called meditation *turiya*,
"the fourth." When you go beyond the deepest sleep and still
you are aware, that awareness is meditation. It is not an experience, it is you, your very being.

But these hi-tech mechanisms can be of tremendous use in the right hands. They can create wavelengths in your mind so that you start feeling relaxed, as if half asleep; thoughts are disappearing and a moment comes that everything becomes silent in you. That is the moment when the waves are of deep sleep. You will not be aware of this deep sleep, but after ten minutes when you are unplugged from the machine you will see the effects: you are calm, quiet, peaceful. No worry, no tension, life seems to be more playful and joyous. One feels as if one has had an inner bath. Your whole being is calm and cool.

With machines, things are very certain because they don't depend on any doing of yours. It is just like listening to music: you feel peaceful, harmonious. Those machines will lead you up to the third state: deep sleep, sleep without dreams.

But if you think this is meditation you are wrong. I will say this is good experience, and while you are in that moment of deep sleep, if you can be aware from the very beginning... As the mind starts changing its waves, you have to be more alert, more awake, more watchful of what is happening, you will see that mind is by and by falling asleep. If you can see the mind falling asleep, the one who is seeing the mind falling asleep is your being. And that is the authentic purpose of all meditation.

These machines cannot create that awareness; that awareness you will have to create. But these machines can certainly create within ten minutes a possibility that you may not be able to create in years of effort. So I am not against these hi-tech instruments, I am all for them. It is just that I want the people who are spreading those machines around the world to know that they are doing good work, but it is incomplete.

It will be complete only when the person in the deepest silence is also alert, like a small flame of awareness which goes on burning. Everything disappears, all around darkness and silence and peace, but an unwavering flame of awareness remains.

In the right hands, the machine can be used and people can be taught that the real thing will not come through the machine. The machine can create the very essential ground in which that flame can grow, but that flame depends on you, not on the machine.

So I am in favor of those machines on the one hand, and on the other hand I am very much against them because many, many people will think this is meditation.

Osho,
After working with the cathartic techniques for some time,
I feel that a deep inner harmony, balance and centering is
happening to me. Is this real or am I imagining it?

It has been my observation that people hanker for silence and when it starts happening, they can't believe it. It is too good to be true. And particularly people who have always condemned themselves: how can they believe that it is happening to them? "Impossible! It may have happened to a Buddha or to a Jesus, but to me? No, it is not possible." They come to me. They are disturbed so much by silence, disturbed that it is happening: "Is it true, or I am imagining it?" Why worry? Even if it is imagination, it is better than imagining anger, it is better than imagining sex, lust.

And I tell you, nobody can imagine silence. Imagination needs some form; silence has no form. Imagination means thinking in images, and silence has no image. You cannot imagine it. There is no possibility. You cannot imagine enlightenment, you cannot imagine satori, samadhi, silence, no. Imagination needs some base, some form, and silence is formless, indefinable. Nobody has ever painted a picture of it; nobody can paint it. Nobody has carved an image of it; nobody can do it.

You cannot imagine silence. The mind is playing tricks. The mind will say, "It must be imagination. How can it be possible for you, such a stupid man as you are, and silence happening to you? You must be imagining it." Or, "This guy Osho has hypnotized you. You must be deceived somewhere." Don't create such problems. Life has enough problems. When silence is happening, enjoy it, celebrate it. It means the chaotic forces have been thrown out. The mind is playing its last game. It plays to the very end; to the very, very end it goes on playing. At the last moment of enlightenment, when it is just going to happen, then too the mind plays the last because it is the last battle.

Don't worry about whether it is real or unreal or whether

chaos will come after it or not. Because by thinking in this way you have already brought the chaos in; it is your idea which can create chaos. And when it is created, the mind will say, "Now listen, I had told you before."

Mind is very self-fulfilling. First it gives you a seed, and when it sprouts the mind says, "Look, I was telling you beforehand that you are deceived." The chaos has come, and it has been brought by the idea. So why bother about the future, whether the chaos is still to come or not, or whether it has passed or not? Right this moment you are silent – why not celebrate it? And I tell you, if you celebrate, it grows.

In this world of consciousness, nothing is as helpful as celebration. Celebration is like watering a plant. Worry is just the opposite of celebration; it is just like cutting off the roots. Feel happy! Dance with your silence. This moment it is there – enough. Why ask for more? Tomorrow will take care of itself. This moment is too much; why not live it, celebrate it, share it, enjoy it? Let it become a song, a dance, a poetry; let it be creative. Let your silence be creative; do something with it.

Millions of things are possible because nothing is more creative than silence. No need to become a very great painter, world famous, a Picasso. No need to become a Henry Moore; no need to become a great poet. Those ambitions of being great are of the mind, not of the silence. In your own way, howsoever small, paint. In your own way, howsoever small, create a haiku. In your own way, howsoever small, sing a song, dance a little, celebrate, and you will find the next moment brings more silence. And once you know that the more you celebrate, the more is given to you... The more you share, the more you become capable of receiving it – each moment it goes on growing, growing. And the next moment is always born out of this moment, so why worry about it? If this moment is silent, how can the next moment be chaos? From where will it come? It is going to be born out of this moment. If I am happy this moment, how can I be unhappy in the next moment?

If you want the next moment to be unhappy, you will have to become unhappy in this moment because out of unhappiness, unhappiness is born; out of happiness, happiness is born. Whatsoever you want to reap in the next moment, you will have

to sow right now. Once the worry is allowed and you start thinking that chaos will come, it will come; you have already brought
it. Now you will have to harvest it; it has already come. No need
to wait for the next moment: it is already there.

Remember this – and this is really something strange –
when you are sad, you never think that it may be imaginary.
I have never come across a man who is sad and who says
to me that maybe it is just imaginary. Sadness is perfectly
real. But happiness? Immediately something goes wrong and
you start thinking, "Maybe it is imaginary." Whenever you are
tense, you never think it is imaginary. If you can think that
your tension and anguish is imaginary, it will disappear. And
if you think your silence and happiness is imaginary, it will
disappear.

Whatsoever is taken as real becomes real. Whatsoever is
taken as unreal becomes unreal. You are the creator of the
whole world around you; remember this. It is so rare to achieve
a moment of happiness, bliss – don't waste it in thinking. But
if you don't do anything, the possibility of worry is there. If you
don't do anything – if you don't dance, if you don't sing, if
you don't share, the possibility is there. The very energy that
could have been creative will create the worry. It will start creating new tensions inside.

Energy has to be creative. If you don't use it for happiness,
the same energy will be used for unhappiness. And you have
such deep-rooted habits for unhappiness that the energy flow is
very loose and natural. For happiness, it is an uphill task.

So for a few days you will have to be constantly aware,
and whenever there is a moment let it grip you, possess you, and
enjoy it in such a totality. How can the next moment be different? From where will it be different? From where will it come?

Your time is created within you. Your time is not my time.
There exist as many parallel times as there are minds. There
is not one time. If there is one time, then there will be difficulty. Then, amidst the whole miserable humankind, nobody
can become a buddha because we belong to the same time.
No, it is not the same.

My time comes from me – it is my creativity. If this moment
is beautiful, the next moment is born more beautiful – this is my

time. If this moment is sad for you, then a sadder moment is born out of you – that is your time. Millions of parallel lines of time exist. And there are a few people who exist without time – those who have attained no-mind. They have no time because they don't think about the past; it is gone, so only fools think about it. When something is gone, it is gone.

There is a Buddhist mantra: "*Gate, gate, paragate – swaha. Gone, gone, absolutely gone; let it go into the fire.*" The past is gone, the future has not come yet. Why worry about it? When it comes, we will see. You will be there to encounter it, so why worry about it? The gone is gone, the not-come has not yet come. Only this moment is left – pure, intense with energy. Live it! If it is silence, be grateful. If it is blissful, thank existence, trust it. And if you can trust, it will grow. If you distrust, you have already poisoned it.

Osho,
When I decide to be aware in work, I forget about awareness. Later, when I become aware that I was not aware, I feel guilty. How can I be aware while working?

It is one of the basic problems for anybody who is trying to be aware while at work – because work demands that you should forget yourself completely. You should be involved in it as deeply as if you are absent. Unless such total involvement is there, the work remains superficial.

All that is great, created by man – in painting, in poetry, in architecture, in sculpture, in any dimension of life – needs you to be totally involved. And if you are trying to be aware at the same time, your work will never be first rate because you will not be in it.

So awareness while you are working needs a tremendous training and discipline, and one has to start from very simple actions. For example, walking: you can walk and you can be aware that you are walking. Each step can be full of awareness. Eating… Just as in Zen monasteries they drink tea; they call it a tea ceremony because sipping tea, one has to remain alert and aware.

These are small actions, but to begin with they are perfectly

good. One should not start with something like painting, dancing – those are very deep and complex phenomena. Start with
small actions of daily routine life. As you become more and
more accustomed to awareness, as awareness becomes just
like breathing – you don't have to make any effort for it, it
has become spontaneous – then in any act, any work, you can
be aware.

But remember the condition: it has to be effortless; it has
to be part of spontaneity. Then painting or composing music,
or dancing, or even fighting an enemy with a sword, you can
remain absolutely aware. But that awareness is not the awareness you are trying to do. It is not the beginning, it is the culmi-
nation of a long discipline.

In everyday life you should follow the simple course. First
become aware about actions which do not need your involvement. You can walk and you can go on thinking; you can eat
and you can go on thinking.

Replace thinking by awareness.

Go on eating and remain alert that you are eating. Walk and
replace thinking by awareness. Go on walking; perhaps your
walking will be a little slower and more graceful. But awareness
is possible with these small acts. And as you become more and
more articulate, use more complicated activities.

A day comes when there is no activity in the world in which
you cannot remain alert and, at the same time, act with totality.

You are saying, "When I decide to be aware in work, I forget about awareness." It has not to be your decision, it has to
be your long discipline. And awareness has to come spontaneously; you are not to call it, you are not to force it.

"And when I become aware that I was not aware, I feel
guilty." That is absolute stupidity. When you become aware that
you were not aware, feel happy that at least now you are aware.
There is no place in my teachings for the concept of guilt.

Guilt is one of the cancers of the soul. And all the religions
have used guilt to destroy your dignity, your pride, and to make
you just slaves. There is no need to feel guilty, it is natural.
Awareness is such a great thing that even if you can be aware
for a few seconds, rejoice. Don't pay attention to those moments
when you forgot. Pay attention to that state when you suddenly

remember, "I was not aware." Feel fortunate that at least after a few hours, awareness has returned. Don't make it into repentance, guilt, sadness, because by being guilty and sad, you are not going to be helped. You will feel, deep down, a failure. And once a feeling of failure settles in you, awareness will become even more difficult.

Change your whole focus. It is great that you became aware that you had forgotten to be aware. Now don't forget, for as long as possible. Again you will forget; again you will remember – but each time, the gap of forgetfulness will become smaller and smaller. If you can avoid guilt, which is basically Christian, your gaps of unawareness will become shorter, and one day they will simply disappear. Awareness will become just like breathing or the heartbeat, or the blood circulating in you – day in, day out.

So be watchful that you don't feel guilty. There is nothing to feel guilty about. It is immensely significant that the trees don't listen to your Catholic priests. Otherwise, they will make the roses feel guilty: "Why do you have thorns?" And the rose, danc-ing in the wind, in the rain, in the sun, will suddenly become sad. The dance will disappear, the joy will disappear, the fra-grance will disappear. Now the thorn will become his only reality, a wound – "Why do you have thorns?"

But because there are no rosebushes as foolish as to listen to a priest of any religion, roses go on dancing, and with the roses, thorns also go on dancing.

The whole existence is guiltless. And a man, the moment he becomes guiltless, becomes part of the universal flow of life.

Whatever you do – if it is not right, don't do it again. If you feel it hurts somebody, don't do it again. But there is no need to feel guilty, there is no need to be repentant, there is no need to do penance and torture yourself.

I want to change your focus completely. Rather than count-ing how many times you forgot to remember to be aware, count those few beautiful moments when you were crystal clear and aware. Those few moments are enough to save you, are enough to cure you, to heal you. And if you pay attention to them, they will go on growing and spreading in your consciousness. Slowly, slowly the whole darkness of unawareness will disappear.

Yes, in the beginning you will find many times that perhaps it was not possible to be working and to be aware together. But I say unto you that it is not only possible, it is very easily possible. Just begin in the right way. Just don't start from *xyz*; start from *abc*.

In life, we go on missing many things because of the wrong start. Everything should be started from the very beginning. Our minds are impatient; we want to do everything quickly. We want to reach the highest point without passing through every rung of the ladder.

But that means an absolute failure. And once you fail in something like awareness – it is not a small failure – perhaps you will not try it again, ever. The failure hurts.

So anything that is as valuable as awareness – because it can open all the doors of the mysteries of existence, it can bring you to the very temple of God – you should start very carefully and from the very beginning. And move very slowly.

Just a little patience and the goal is not far away.

Osho,
I have been having wonderful experiences when I meditate,
but I feel there is something I am missing. What is it?

One of the most fundamental things to remember is that whatever you come across in your inner journey, you are not it. You are the one who is witnessing it. It may be nothingness, it may be blissfulness, it may be silence, but one thing has to be remembered – however beautiful and however enchanting an experience you come to, you are not it. You are the one who is experiencing it.

And if you go on and on and on, the ultimate in the journey is the point when there is no experience left – neither silence, nor blissfulness, nor nothingness. There is nothing as an object for you, but only your subjectivity. The mirror is empty, it is not reflecting anything. It is you.

Even great travelers of the inner world have been stuck in beautiful experiences, and have become identified with those experiences thinking, "I have found myself." They have stopped before reaching the final stage where all experiences disappear.

Osho,
Is there a way to learn to watch? And what do I watch?

One has to start watching the body walking, sitting, going to bed, eating. One should start from the most solid because it is easier. And then one should move to subtler experiences. One should start watching thoughts. And when one becomes an expert in watching thoughts, then one should start watching feelings. After you feel that you can watch your feelings, then you should start watching your moods, which are even more subtle than your feelings, and vaguer.

The miracle of watching is that as you are watching the body, your watcher is becoming stronger; as you are watching the thoughts, your watcher is becoming stronger; as you are watching the feelings, the watcher is becoming even stronger. When you are watching your moods, the watcher is so strong that it can remain watching itself, just as a candle in the dark night not only lights everything around it, it also lights itself.

To find the watcher in its purity is the greatest achievement in spirituality because the watcher in you is your very soul, the watcher in you is your immortality. But never for a single moment think "I have it," because that is the moment when you miss.

Watching is an eternal process; you always go on becoming deeper and deeper, but you never come to the end where you can say "I have it." In fact, the deeper you go, the more you become aware that you have entered a process which is eternal – without any beginning and without any end.

But people are watching only others; they never bother to watch themselves. Everybody is watching – that is the most superficial watching – what the other person is doing, what the other person is wearing, how he looks. Everybody is watching; watching is not something new to be introduced in your life. It has only to be deepened, taken away from others and arrowed toward your own inner feelings, thoughts, moods – and finally, the watcher itself.

A Jew is sitting in a train opposite a priest.

"Tell me, your worship, why do you wear your collar back to front?"

"Because I am a father," answers the priest.

"I am also a father, and I don't wear my collar like that," says the Jew.

"Ah," says the priest, "but I am a father to thousands."

"Then maybe," replies the Jew, "it is your trousers you should wear back to front."

People are very watchful about everybody else...

Two Polacks went out for a walk when suddenly it began to rain. "Quick," said one man, "open your umbrella."

"It won't help," said his friend, "my umbrella is full of holes."

"Then why did you bring it in the first place?"

"I did not think it would rain."

You can laugh very easily about ridiculous acts of people, but have you ever laughed about yourself? Have you ever caught yourself doing something ridiculous? No, you keep yourself completely unwatched; all your watching is of others, and that is not of any help.

Use this energy of watchfulness for a transformation of your being. It can bring you so much bliss and so much benediction that you cannot even dream of it. A simple process, but once you start using it on yourself, it becomes a meditation.

One can make meditations out of anything.

Anything that leads you to yourself is meditation. And it is immensely significant to find your own meditation because in the very finding you will find great joy. Because it is your own finding – not some ritual imposed upon you – you will love to go deeper into it. The deeper you go into it, the happier you will feel – peaceful, more silent, more together, more dignified, more graceful.

You all know watching, so there is no question of learning it, it is just a question of changing the objects of watching. Bring them closer.

Watch your body, and you will be surprised. I can move my hand without watching, and I can move my hand with watching. You will not see the difference, but I can feel the difference. When I move it with watchfulness, there is a grace and beauty in it, a peacefulness, and a silence. You can walk, watching each step; it will give you all the benefit that walking can give you as an exercise, plus it will give you the benefit of a great simple meditation.

Osho,
I've heard you say that the mind should be the servant
instead of our master. But the question still arises: Is there
anything to do with this unruly servant but to watch it? Is
witnessing enough?

There is nothing to do with this unruly servant but just to watch. It appears too simple a solution for too complex a problem, but these are part of the mysteries of existence. The problem may be complex; the solution can be very simple.

Watching, witnessing, being aware, seem to be small words to solve the whole complexity of mind. Millions of years of heritage, tradition, conditioning, prejudice – how will they disappear just by watching?

But they disappear because as Gautam Buddha used to say, "If the lights of the house are on, thieves don't come close to that house, knowing that the master is awake." Because the light is showing from the windows, from the doors, you can see that the light is on. It is not the time to enter the house. When the lights are off, thieves are attracted to the house. Darkness becomes an invitation. As Gautam Buddha used to say, the same is the situation for your thoughts, imaginations, dreams, anxieties – your whole mind.

If the witness is there, the witness is almost like the light: the thieves start dispersing. And if these thieves find there is no witness, they start calling their brothers and cousins and everybody, "Come on!"

It is as simple a phenomenon as light. The moment you bring the light in, the darkness disappears. You don't ask, "Is just light enough for darkness to disappear?" or, "When we have brought the light, will we have to do something more for the darkness to disappear?"

No, just the presence of light is the absence of darkness, and the absence of light is the presence of darkness. The presence of the witness is the absence of the mind, and the absence of the witness is the presence of the mind.

The moment you start watching, slowly, slowly as your watcher becomes stronger, your mind will become weaker. The moment it realizes that the watcher has come to maturity, the mind immediately submits as a beautiful servant. It is a mechanism. If the master has arrived, then the machine can be used. If the master is not there or is fast asleep, then the machine goes on working things – whatsoever it can – on its own. There is nobody to give orders; there is nobody to say, "No, stop! That must not be done."

Then the mind is slowly convinced that it itself is the master. And for thousands of years it has remained your master, so when you try to be a witness it fights because it is a question of it having completely forgotten that it is only a servant. You have been absent so long that it does not recognize you; hence the struggle between the witness and the thoughts.

But the final victory is going to be yours because both nature and existence want you to be the master and the mind to be the servant. Then things are in harmony. Then the mind cannot go wrong. Then everything is existentially relaxed, silent, flowing toward its destiny.

You don't have to do anything but to watch.

Paddy bought a parrot at an auction. He asked the auctioneer, "I have spent a great deal of money on this parrot – are you sure he can talk?"

The auctioneer replied, "Of course I am sure. He was bidding against you."

Such is the unawareness of the mind, and such are the stupidities of the mind.

I have heard that the Irish atheists, seeing that the theists have started a dial-a-prayer service, have also started one! They are atheists, but the competitive mind... They have also started a dial-a-prayer service. When you phone them, nobody answers.

Two tramps were sitting by a campfire one night. One of them was very depressed. "You know Jim," he mused, "the life of a tramp is not as great as it is made out to be. Nights on park benches or in a cold barn, traveling on foot and always dodging the police, being kicked from one town to another, wondering where your next meal is coming from, being sneered at by your fellow man..." His voice trailed off and he sighed heavily.

"Well," said the other tramp, "if that is how you feel about it, why don't you go and find yourself a job?"

"What!" asked the first tramp in amazement, "And admit that I'm a failure?"

Mind has become accustomed to being a master. It will take a little time to bring it to its senses. Witnessing is enough. It is a very silent process, but the consequences are tremendously great. There is no method better than witnessing as far as dispersing the darkness of the mind is concerned.

In fact, there are 112 methods of meditation. I have gone through all those methods – and not intellectually. It took me years to go through each method and to find out its very essence. And after going through 112 methods, I was amazed that the essence is witnessing. The methods' nonessentials are different, but the center of each method is witnessing.

For more FAQs, see www.osho.com/meditation

PART II

THE MEDITATIONS

8

OSHO ACTIVE MEDITATIONS

People ask me why I teach active meditations:
it is the only way to find inaction.
Dance to the uttermost, dance in a frenzy, dance madly, and
if your whole energy is involved in it, a moment comes when
suddenly you see the dance is happening on its own –
there is no effort in it.
It is action without action.

Why active meditation?

All OSHO Active Meditations involve action – sometimes intense and physical, sometimes more gentle – followed by inaction, stillness. Some of the meditations are recommended for particular times of the day. All are accompanied by music that has been especially composed to support the different stages.

If you can sit, there is no need for meditations. In Japan, for meditation they have the word *zazen*. It means just sitting, doing nothing. If you can sit, not doing anything, this is the ultimate in meditations. There is no need for anything else.

But can you sit? There is the crux of the whole problem. Can you sit? Can you just sit, doing nothing? If that is possible just sit, do nothing – everything settles by itself, everything simply flows by itself. You are not needed to do anything. But the problem is can you sit?

—

You can move into passivity only when all the junk has been thrown out. Anger has been thrown out, greed has been thrown out, layer upon layer. These things are there, but once you have thrown them out, you can easily slip in. There is no hindrance.

And suddenly, the bright light of the buddha land. Suddenly you are in a totally different world – the world of the lotus law, the world of dharma, the world of Tao.

—

Meditation is an energy phenomenon and one very basic thing has to be understood about all types of energies: energy moves in a dual polarity. That is the only way it moves; there is no other way of its movement. It moves in a dual polarity.

For any energy to become dynamic, the anti-pole is needed. It is just like electricity moving with negative and positive polarities. If there is only negative polarity, electricity will not happen; or if there is only positive polarity, electricity will not happen. Both poles are needed. And when the poles meet, they create electricity; then the spark comes.

And this is so for all types of phenomena. It is how life goes on: between man and woman, the polarity. The woman is the negative life-energy; man is the positive pole. They are electrical – hence so much attraction. With man alone, life would disappear; with woman alone there could be no life, only death. Between man and woman there exists a balance. Between man and woman – these two poles, these two banks – flows the river of life.

Wherever you look, you will find the same energy moving in polarities, balancing itself.

This polarity is very meaningful for meditation because mind is logical and life is dialectical. When I say mind is logical, it means mind moves in a line. When I say life is dialectical, it means life moves with the opposite, not in a line. It zigzags from negative to positive, positive to negative, negative to positive. It zigzags; it uses the opposites.

Mind moves in a line, a simple straight line. It never moves to the opposite – it denies the opposite. It believes in one, and life believes in two.

So whatsoever the mind creates, it always chooses the one. If the mind chooses silence – if the mind has become fed up with all the noise that is created in life, it decides to be silent – then it goes to the Himalayas. It wants to be silent, it doesn't want anything to do with any type of noise. Even the song of the birds will disturb it; the breeze blowing through the trees will be a disturbance. The mind wants silence; it has chosen the line. Now the opposite has to be denied completely.

But a man living in the Himalayas – seeking silence, avoiding the other, the opposite – will become dead; he will certainly become dull. And the more he chooses to be silent, the duller he will become because life needs the opposite, the challenge of the opposite.

There is a different type of silence which exists between two opposites.

The first is a dead silence, the silence of the cemetery. A dead man is silent, but you would not like to be a dead man. A dead man is absolutely silent. Nobody can disturb him, his concentration is perfect. You cannot do anything to distract his mind; his mind is absolutely fixed. Even if the whole world goes mad all around, he will remain in his concentration. But still you would not like to be a dead man. Silence, concentration, or whatever it is called... You would not like to be dead because if you are silent and dead, the silence is meaningless.

Silence must happen while you are absolutely alive, vital, bubbling with life and energy. Then silence is meaningful. But the silence will have a different, altogether different quality to it. It will not be dull. It will be alive. It will be a subtle balance between two polarities. Do much, but don't be a doer – then you achieve both. Move in the world, but don't be a part of it. Live in the world, but don't let the world live in you. Then the contradiction has been absorbed. Then you are not rejecting anything, not denying anything. Then the whole of existence has been accepted. And that's what I'm doing. Dynamic Meditation is a contradiction. *Dynamic* means effort, much effort, absolute effort. And *meditation* means silence, no effort, no activity. You can call it a dialectical meditation.

When you are doing the chaotic Dynamic Meditation or the Kundalini or the Nadabrahma, these are not really meditations. You are just getting in tune. It is just like when Indian classical musicians play: for half an hour, or sometimes even longer, they simply go on preparing their instruments. They move the knobs, they make the strings tight or loose, and the drummer will go on checking whether his drum is perfect or not. They go on doing this for half an hour; it is not music, it is just preparation. My Kundalini Meditation is not really meditation, it is just preparation. You are preparing your instrument. When it is ready, you come to silence, meditation starts. You are utterly there. You have woken yourself up by jumping, by dancing, by breathing, by shouting – these are all devices to make you a little more alert than you ordinarily are. Once you are alert, then the waiting.

Waiting is meditation – waiting with full awareness. And then it comes; it descends on you, it surrounds you, it plays around you, it dances around you. It cleanses you, it purifies you, it transforms you.

Why use music?
Much of the music to support the OSHO Active Meditations has been composed under Osho's direction, and with his instruction that once finalized, the music should remain the same, not changed in any way.

*He explained that its effect in the meditation will create and expand
its own energy field over time as it connects with more people, and
that over a thousand years the music will form a field of resonance
that will deeply affect each person doing the meditation.*

*The music indicates the beginning of each new phase of the medita-
tions and energetically supports each stage. For further details, see
Appendix II.*

To me, music and meditation are two aspects of the same
phenomenon. And without music, meditation lacks something;
without music, meditation is a little dull, unalive. Without meditation, music is simply noise – harmonious, but noise. Without
meditation, music is an entertainment. And without music, meditation becomes more and more negative, tends to be death-
oriented.

Hence my insistence that music and meditation should go
together. That adds a new dimension to both. Both are enriched
by it.

Music helps you from the outside to fall in tune with the inner.
Music is a device; it was invented by the buddhas. All that is
beautiful in the world, all that is valuable in the world has always
been discovered by the buddhas. Only they can discover because
they have traveled the inner country, the inner, immeasurable
universe. Whatsoever they have found in the inner world, whatsoever they have experienced in the inner world, they have tried
to make something similar on the outside for those who can only
understand that which is objective; for those who are not yet able
to enter the interiority of their own being, who are not yet even
aware that there is an inner world. Devices can be created on the
outside which can help.

One can have a kind of peace which is like death: you are
not tense, you are not disturbed, but you are not celebrating
either. And that's the cheapest way to attain peace: just dull
yourself, slowly, slowly become more and more insensitive, and
one day there is a kind of peace.

That's what happens in the monasteries; that's what you will
find in the so-called saints: they are peaceful but the peace has

no value in it. It is the peace of the cemetery, not the peace of a garden. Peace has to be blissful. It should be vibrant. It should not be just an absence of noise; it should be the presence of music. And that's my whole approach toward meditation.

OSHO DYNAMIC MEDITATION

This meditation is a fast, intense, and thorough way to break old, ingrained patterns in the bodymind that keep one imprisoned in the past, and to experience the freedom, the witnessing, silence and peace that are hidden behind those prison walls.

The meditation is meant to be done in the early morning, when "the whole of nature becomes alive, the night has gone, the sun is coming up and everything becomes conscious and alert."

You can do this meditation alone, but to start with it can be helpful to do it with other people. It is an individual experience, so remain oblivious of others around you. Wear loose, comfortable clothing.

This meditation is to be done with its specific OSHO Dynamic Meditation music, which indicates and energetically supports the different stages. For further details, see Appendix II.

It takes time – at least three weeks are needed to get the feel of it, and three months to move into a different world. But that too is not fixed. It differs from individual to individual. If your intensity is very great, it can even happen in three days.

INSTRUCTIONS
The meditation lasts one hour and has five stages. Keep your eyes closed throughout, using a blindfold if necessary.

This is a meditation in which you have to be continuously alert, conscious, aware, whatsoever you do. Remain a witness. And when – in the fourth stage – you have become completely inactive, frozen, then this alertness will come to its peak.

FIRST STAGE: 10 MINUTES
Breathing chaotically through the nose, let the breathing be intense, deep, fast, without rhythm, with no pattern – and concentrating always on the exhalation. The body will take care of the inhalation. The breath should move deeply into the lungs. Do this as fast and as hard as you possibly can, until you literally become the breathing. Use your natural body movements to help you to build up your energy. Feel it building up, but don't let go during the first stage.

SECOND STAGE: 10 MINUTES
EXPLODE! Let go of everything that needs to be thrown out. Follow your body. Give your body freedom to express whatever is there. Go totally mad. Scream, shout, cry, jump, kick, shake, dance, sing, laugh; throw yourself around. Hold nothing back; keep your whole body moving. A little acting often helps to get you started. Never allow your mind to interfere with what is happening. Consciously go mad. Be total.

THIRD STAGE: 10 MINUTES
With arms raised high above your head, jump up and down shouting the mantra, "Hoo! Hoo! Hoo!" as deeply as possible. Each time you land, on the flats of your feet, let the sound hammer deep into the sex center. Give all you have: exhaust yourself completely.

FOURTH STAGE: 15 MINUTES
STOP! Freeze wherever you are, in whatever position you find yourself. Don't arrange the body in any way. A cough, a movement, anything, will dissipate the energy flow and the effort will be lost. Be a witness to everything that is happening to you.

FIFTH STAGE: 15 MINUTES
Celebrate! With music and dance, express whatsoever is there. Carry your aliveness with you throughout the day.

Note: If your meditation space prevents you from making noise, you can do this silent alternative: rather than throwing out the sounds, let the catharsis in the second stage take place entirely through bodily movements. In the third stage, the sound Hoo! can be hammered silently inside, and the fifth stage can become an expressive dance.

This first meditation is a meditation in which you have to be continuously alert, conscious, aware, whatsoever you do: the first step, breathing; the second step, catharsis; the third step, the mantra, the *mahamantra, hoo.*

Remain a witness. Don't get lost.

It is easy to get lost. While you are breathing you can forget: you can become one with the breathing so much that you can forget the witness. But then you miss the point. Breathe as fast, as deep as possible, bring your total energy to it, but still remain a witness.

Observe what is happening as if you are just a spectator; as if the whole thing is happening to somebody else; as if the whole thing is happening in the body, and the consciousness is just centered and looking.

This witnessing has to be carried in all three steps. And when everything stops, and in the fourth step you have become completely inactive, frozen, then this alertness will come to its peak.

—

Someone has said that the meditation we are doing here seems to be sheer madness. It is! And it is that way for a purpose. It is madness with a method; it is consciously chosen.

Remember, you cannot go mad voluntarily. Madness takes possession of you. Only then can you go mad. If you go mad voluntarily, that's a totally different thing. You are basically in control, and one who can control even his madness will never go mad.

—

We have done so much violence to our bodies. So in this chaotic meditation, I am forcing your bodies to be alive again. Many blocks will be broken; many settled things unsettled again; many systems will become liquid again. There will be pain, but welcome it. It is a blessing and you will overcome it. Continue! There is no need to think what to do. Simply continue the meditation. I have seen hundreds and hundreds of people passing through the same process. Within a few days the pain is gone. And when the pain is gone, you will have a subtle joy around your body.

You cannot have it right now because the pain is there. You may know it or you may not know it, but the pain is there all over your body. You have simply become unconscious about it because it has always been with you. Whatsoever is always there, you become unconscious about. Through meditation you will become conscious and then the mind will say, "Don't do this; the whole body is aching." Don't listen to the mind. Simply go on doing it.

Within a certain period the pain will be thrown out. When the pain is thrown out, your body has again become receptive and there is no block, no poisons around it, you will always have a subtle feeling of joy wrapped around you.

The first step is ten minutes of fast, chaotic breathing with no system. This is not a yoga exercise: it is chaotic, anarchic. Why? – because if you use any systematic breathing, any rhythm, the mind can control it. The mind can control any system; the mind is the great systematizer. We are here to break the system, the system of the mind. So breathe chaotically, like a madman – fast. Take the breath in as much as you can and throw it out – take it in and throw it out fast, with no rhythm, so that the mind is just shocked. Breathing is a great device to shock the mind.

You must remember that with every emotion, the breathing changes. Every emotion has its own system of breathing. When you are in love, the breathing is relaxed; when you are angry, the breathing can never be relaxed. When you hate someone, the breathing is one thing; when you are in compassion, the breathing is different. When you are at ease, the breathing is so silent that you cannot even feel it; when you are tense, the breathing cannot be silent – you can feel it.

This chaotic breathing belongs to no emotion. So simply by doing it you transcend emotions, the mechanism of the mind. And the mind is just thrown off; it cannot continue. Ten minutes of mad, fast breathing.

The more oxygen in the body, the more alive you become, the more animal-like. Animals are alive and man is half dead, half alive. You have to be made into an animal again. Only then can something higher develop in you. You are false and if you are only half alive, nothing can be done with you. So this chaotic breathing will make you like an animal: alive, vibrating, vital – with more oxygen in your blood, more energy in your cells. Your body cells will become more alive. This oxygenation helps to create body electricity – or you can call it *bioenergy*. When there is electricity in the body, you can move deep within, beyond yourself.

Then my second step is a catharsis. I tell you to be consciously insane and whatever comes to your mind – *whatever*

– allow it expression, cooperate with it. No resistance; just a flow of emotions.

If you want to scream, then scream. Cooperate with it. A deep scream, a total scream in which your whole being becomes involved, is very therapeutic, deeply therapeutic. Many things, many diseases, will be released just by the scream. If the scream is total, your whole being will be in it. Allow yourself expression through crying, dancing, weeping, jumping – "freaking out" as they say. This second step is also for ten minutes, and within a few days you will come to feel what it is.

In the beginning it may just be forced, an effort, or it may even be just acting. We have become so false that nothing real or authentic can be done by us. We have not laughed, we have not cried, we have not screamed authentically. Everything is just a facade, a mask. So when you begin to do it, in the beginning it may be forced. It may need effort; there may be just acting. But do not bother about it. Go on. Soon you will touch those sources where you have repressed many things. You will touch those sources and once they are released, you will feel unburdened. A new life will come to you; a new birth will take place.

This unburdening is basic and without it there can be no meditation for man as he is. I am not talking about the exceptions. They are irrelevant.

With this second step – when things are thrown out – you become vacant. And this is what is meant by emptiness: to be empty of all repressions. Then in this emptiness something can be done.

In the third step I use the sound, hoo. Many sounds have been used in the past. Each sound has something specific to do. For example, Hindus have been using the sound, aum. This may be familiar to you. But I won't suggest aum. It never goes deeper than the heart. It just touches the heart and moves back; it cannot go deeper.

Sufis have used hoo, and if you say hoo loudly, it goes deep to the sex center. So this sound is used just as a hammering within. When you have become vacant and empty, only then can this sound move within you.

The movement of the sound is possible only when you are empty. If you are filled with repressions, nothing will happen.

And sometimes it is even dangerous to use a mantra or sound when you are filled with repressions.

So only in the third step, for ten minutes, is this *hoo* to be used – as loudly as possible. Bring your total energy to it. This is a hammering. When you are empty, this *hoo* goes deep down and hits the sex center.

The sex center can be hit in two ways. The first way is naturally. Whenever you are attracted to a member of the opposite sex, the sex center is hit from without. And in reality that hit is also a subtle vibration. A man is attracted to a woman or a woman is attracted to a man. Why are they attracted? What is there in a man and what is there in a woman to account for it? – a positive or negative electricity hits them, a subtle vibration. It is a sound, really. You may have observed that birds use sound for sex appeal. All their singing is sexual. They are repeatedly hitting each other with particular sounds. These sounds hit the sex centers of birds of the opposite sex.

Subtle vibrations of electricity are hitting you from without. When your sex center is hit from without, your energy begins to flow outward. That causes reproduction, birth. Someone else will be born out of you.

This *hoo* is hitting the same center of energy, but from within. And when the sex center is hit from within, the energy starts to flow within. This inner flow of energy changes you completely. You become transformed: you give birth to yourself.

You are transformed only when your energy moves in a totally opposite direction. Right now it is flowing out, but then it begins to flow within. Now it is flowing down, but then it flows upward. This upward flow of energy is what is known as kundalini. You will feel it actually flowing in your spine and the higher it moves, the higher you will move with it. When this energy reaches your head center, the last, the seventh center, you are the highest man possible.

In the third step, I use *hoo* as a vehicle to bring your energy upward. These first three steps are cathartic. They are not really meditation, but just preparation for it. They are a "getting ready" to take the jump, not the jump itself. The fourth step is the jump.

In the fourth step, I tell you just to be a witness – a conscious alertness; not doing anything, but just remaining a witness, just remaining with yourself. Not doing anything – no movement, no desire, no becoming, but just remaining then and there, silently witnessing whatsoever is happening.

That remaining in the center, in yourself, is possible because of the first three steps. Unless those three are done you cannot remain with yourself. You can go on talking about it, thinking about it, dreaming about it, but it will not happen because you are not ready.

Those first three steps will make you ready to remain with the moment, they will make you aware. That is meditation, and in that meditation something happens that is beyond words. And once it happens you will never be the same again; it is impossible. It is a growth. It is not simply an experience, it is a growth.

The energy simply moves upward and you are not to do anything. That's why I go on emphasizing not to move. After the third step when I say "Stop!" stop completely. Don't do anything at all because anything can become a diversion and you miss the point. Anything, just a cough or a sneeze, and you may miss the whole thing because the mind has become diverted and the flow will stop immediately because your attention has moved.

Don't do anything. You are not going to die. Even if the sneeze is coming and you don't sneeze for ten minutes, you will not die. If you feel like coughing, if you feel an irritation in the throat and you don't do anything, you are not going to die.

Right this moment you are silent – why not celebrate it? And I tell you, if you celebrate, it grows.

In this world of consciousness, nothing is as helpful as celebration. Celebration is like watering a plant. Worry is just the opposite of celebration; it is just like cutting the roots. Feel happy! Dance with your silence. This moment it is there – enough. Why ask for more? Tomorrow will take care of itself. This moment is too much; why not live it, celebrate it, share it, enjoy it?

Dynamic meditation is not just a catharsis. The catharsis is to create a space for silence, peace, love, meditativeness. This is the positive side. The negative side is okay, but the purpose is to create that space. Dynamic is in three parts: catharsis, silence, bliss.

Recommended reading:
Osho, The New Alchemy: To Turn You On
Osho, The Supreme Doctrine

OSHO KUNDALINI MEDITATION

This "sister meditation" to the OSHO Dynamic is best done at sunset or in the late afternoon. Being fully immersed in the shaking and dancing of the first two stages helps to "melt" the rocklike being, wherever the energy flow has been repressed and blocked. Then that energy can flow, dance and be transformed into bliss and joy. The last two stages enable all this energy to flow vertically, to move upward into silence. It is a highly effective way of unwinding and letting go at the end of the day.

This meditation is to be done with its specific OSHO Kundalini Meditation music, which indicates and energetically supports the different stages. For further details, see Appendix II.

INSTRUCTIONS
The meditation lasts one hour and has four stages.

FIRST STAGE: 15 MINUTES
Be loose and let your whole body shake, feeling the energies moving up from your feet. Let go everywhere and become the shaking. Your eyes may be open or closed.

SECOND STAGE: 15 MINUTES
Dance – any way you feel, and let the whole body move as it wishes. Your eyes may be open or closed.

THIRD STAGE: 15 MINUTES
Close your eyes and be still, sitting or standing – witnessing whatever is happening inside and out.

FOURTH STAGE: 15 MINUTES
Keeping your eyes closed, lie down and be still.

Note: In the fourth stage you may choose to remain sitting if you wish.

If you are doing the Kundalini Meditation, allow the shaking, don't *do* it! Stand silently, feel it coming and when your body starts a little trembling, help it, but don't *do* it. Enjoy it, feel blissful about it, allow it, receive it, welcome it, but don't will it. If you force it, it will become an exercise, a physical exercise of the body. Then the shaking will be there, but just on the surface. It will not penetrate you. You will remain solid, stone-like, rocklike within. You will remain the manipulator, the doer, and the body will just be following. The body is not the question – *you* are the question.

When I say shake, I mean your solidity, your rocklike being should shake to the very foundations, so it becomes liquid, fluid, melts, flows. And when the rocklike being becomes liquid your body will follow. Then there is no shaker, only shaking; then nobody is doing it, it is simply happening. Then the doer is not.

There is no need to awaken the kundalini, the energy pool that is like a coiled serpent. We do Kundalini Meditation here, but the purpose is not to awaken the kundalini; the purpose is something different. The purpose is to give a dance to the kundalini energy that is within you.

The purpose is very different. The energy that is inside you is, as yet, asleep. So it should either be awakened... And to awaken it you will have to impact it, shake it. My own experience is that there is no need to awaken it; it should just be given a dance; it should just be made musical; it should just be transformed into a blissful celebration. So there is no need to push it or jolt it.

When Nijinsky used to dance, sometimes it would happen that he would make such a high leap that it would be against all the laws of gravitation. Scientists were puzzled: this was not possible. Such a high jump was not possible; it *should* not be possible because the law of gravitation does not allow you to leap that high. But what was even more miraculous was that after making such a high jump, he would come back down to the stage as slowly as a bird's feather – slowly, swaying, floating in the air. That too was very paradoxical. Gravitation pulls things down very fast; things come down like a falling stone, not like a feather.

Whenever Nijinsky was asked how he managed to do this, he would say, "That is exactly what I am also wondering! But it is not right to say that I do it; it just happens. Whenever I try to do it, it never happens. It only happens sometimes, when I am not trying to do it at all, when I am absorbed in the dance – so absorbed that my ego is totally dissolved. Then, this phenomenon takes place."

Nijinsky was unknowingly reaching the state that I want to take you to through Kundalini Meditation. The purpose of my Kundalini Meditation is not that which has been there for centuries. As far as I am concerned, I am changing the purpose of everything. Here, Kundalini Meditation means: dance, be soaked in bliss, become immersed. Become so immersed that your ego does not remain separate. That's all. Then, something will happen inside you, you will suddenly be out of the grip of gravitation. And you will suddenly find that there is such silence permeating within you, such virgin silence, as you have never known before. You will be melted in bliss. And when you come back, you will be altogether a different person.

This is not the old traditional process of awakening the kundalini. This is the process of imparting a dance to the kundalini. It is something very different altogether.

—

Note: In the following passage, "the first door" indicates the lowest chakra or energy center and "the tenth door," the highest chakra or energy center.

The second stage is dancing. Dancing means the energy that has now spread everywhere gets transformed into bliss. Dance as if you are celebrating, as if something tremendous has happened, as if a light has descended into your life. Dance with joy because the more blissful you are, the more energy moves upward; the more energy moves upward, the more blissful you become. Suppose you were intoxicated and started dancing as if you had drunk the entire tavern dry, would you dance like a miser? It wouldn't happen. Dancing like a miser would mean dancing as if you have to do it: "What to do, I just got caught here..." Or as if you are just observing, expecting that perhaps something will happen by dancing this way! No, that won't work. Such lukewarm efforts won't work. You need intense passion! Dance like a madman.

Without madness you cannot attain the ultimate. If you move

with your mind, then you will remain where you are. You need to go a little beyond your mind. And when your whole energy becomes ecstatic, when it begins to flow upward… To be ecstatic means the energy is moving upward because a feeling of joy and bliss is experienced when the energy has begun to flow vertically. The more it flows downward, the more one feels miserable, the more life descends into hell. That's why we say hell is below and heaven is above. It simply means that hell is connected with the first door and heaven is connected with the tenth door – *above* and *below* mean nothing else.

When your energy falls down to the first door, you create hell for yourself. And when, at the tenth door, your energy flows toward the limitless, you have created a heaven for yourself. Both are hidden within you. When the energy is flowing and you are blissful, stop and either remain standing or sit down so that the energy has a total opportunity to flow. It is useful to sit, so that only the spine remains; the whole body disappears and only the spine remains. The energy moves upward through the spine and all the energy gathers in the spine. Then just lie down, so that it becomes even easier for the gathered energy that is flowing upward to start knocking on the tenth door.

The whole experiment of Kundalini Meditation is all about knocking on the tenth door.

OSHO NADABRAHMA MEDITATION

Nadabrahma is the humming meditation – through humming and hand movements, conflicting parts of you start falling in tune, and you bring harmony to your whole being. Then, with body and mind totally together, you "slip out of their hold" and become a witness to both. This watching from the outside is what brings peace, silence, and bliss.

This meditation is to be done with its specific OSHO Nadabrahma Meditation music, which indicates and energetically supports the different stages. For further details, see Appendix II.

INSTRUCTIONS
The meditation lasts one hour, and has three stages. Your eyes remain closed throughout.

FIRST STAGE: 30 MINUTES
Sit in a relaxed position with eyes closed and lips together. Start humming – loud enough so that if anyone were sitting close to you, they would be able to hear it – and create a vibration throughout your body. You can visualize a hollow tube or an empty vessel, filled only with the vibrations of the humming. A point will come when the humming continues by itself and you become the listener. There is no special breathing and you can alter the pitch or move your body smoothly and slowly if you feel it happening naturally.

SECOND STAGE: 15 MINUTES
The second stage is divided into two 7½-minute sections. For the first half move the hands, palms up, in an outward circular motion. Starting at the navel, both hands move forward and then divide to make two large circles mirroring each other left and right. The movement should be so slow that at times there will appear to be no movement at all. Feel that you are giving energy outward to the universe.

When the music changes after 7½ minutes, turn the hands palms down and start moving them in the opposite direction. Now the hands will come together toward the navel and divide outward to the sides of the body. Feel that you are taking energy in.

As in the first stage, don't inhibit any soft, slow movements of the rest of your body.

THIRD STAGE: 15 MINUTES
Now stop the hand movements and just sit relaxed.

OSHO NADABRAHMA MEDITATION FOR COUPLES

A variation of this technique exists for couples. While both are humming, harmony and sensitivity arises between them and by and by they become intuitive, both functioning on one wavelength.

INSTRUCTIONS
Partners sit facing each other, covered by a sheet and holding each other's crossed hands. It is best to wear no further clothing. Light the room only with four small candles and burn incense which is kept only for this meditation.
Close your eyes and hum together for 30 minutes. After a short while the energies will be felt to meet, merge and unite.

Nadabrahma is a mantra meditation, and mantra is one of the most potent methods. It is very simple yet tremendously effective because when you chant a mantra or you chant a sound, your body starts vibrating; your brain cells particularly start vibrating.

If rightly done your whole brain becomes tremendously vibrant, and the whole body also. Once the body starts vibrating and your mind is already chanting, they fall in tune – a harmony which is ordinarily never there between the two.

Your mind goes on its way, your body continues on its own. The body goes on eating, the mind goes on thinking. The body goes on walking on the road and the mind is moving far away in the stars. They never meet – they each go on separate pathways, and that creates a split.

The basic schizophrenia is created because the body goes in one direction and the mind goes in another direction. And you are the third element – you are neither the body nor the mind, so you are pulled apart by these two. Half of your being is pulled by the body and half of your being is pulled by your mind. So there is great anguish – one feels torn apart.

This is how the mechanism works in a mantra meditation – in Nadabrahma or any chanting – when you start chanting a sound. And any sound will do, even abracadabra... If you start resounding inside, the body starts responding. Sooner or later a moment comes when the body and the mind are together in one direction for the first time. When body and mind are together, you are free from the body and the mind; you are not torn apart. Then the third element which you are in reality – call it soul, spirit, atman, anything – that third element is at ease because it is not being pulled in different directions.

The body and the mind are so engrossed in chanting that the soul can slip out of them very easily, unobserved, and can become a witness, can stand outside and look at the whole game that is going on between the mind and the body. It is such a beautiful rhythm that the mind and body never become aware that the soul has slipped out. They don't allow that so easily, they keep their possession! Nobody wants to lose his possession. The body wants to dominate the soul, the mind wants to dominate the soul.

This is a very sly way to get out of their hold. They become drunk with the chanting and you slip out.

So in Nadabrahma, remember this: let the body and mind be totally together, but remember that you have to become a witness. Get out of them, easily, slowly, from the back door, with no fight, with no struggle. They are drinking: you get out and watch from the outside.

This is the meaning of the English word *ecstasy* – to stand outside. Stand outside and watch from there. It is tremendously peaceful; it is silence, it is bliss, it is benediction.

This is the whole secret of chanting, that's why chanting has prevailed down the centuries. There has never been a religion that has not used chanting and mantra. But there is a danger also. If you don't get outside, if you don't become a witness, there is danger – then you have missed the whole point. If you become drunk with the body and the mind and your soul also becomes drunk, then chanting is an intoxicant. Then it is like a tranquilizer: it will give you a good sleep, that's all. It is a lullaby. Good – nothing wrong in it – but not of any real value either.

So this is the pitfall to be remembered: chanting is so beautiful that one wants to get lost. If you are lost, then good, you enjoyed a rhythm, an inner rhythm, and it was beautiful and you liked it, but it was like a drug – it is an acid trip. By chanting, by the sound, you created certain drugs in your body.

Chanting creates chemical changes in the body, and those changes are no different than marijuana or LSD. Someday, when research goes deeper into meditation, they are going to find that chanting creates chemical changes, just as fasting also creates chemical changes.

After the seventh or eighth day of fasting, one feels tremendously jubilant, weightless, very glad for no reason, delighted – as if all burden has disappeared. Your body is creating a certain chemical change.

I am as much against LSD as I am against fasting. And if chanting is used as a drug, I am against it. So the point to be remembered is that you have not to use the sound, the chanting, the mantra, as an intoxicant for your being. Let it be an intoxicant for the body and the mind, but you slip out of it before you become intoxicated; you stand outside and you watch. You see the body swaying and you see the mind feeling very, very peaceful and calm and quiet. Watch from the outside and be alert like a flame.

If this is not done, you will have a good sleep but nothing more. Then it is a good thing for the health but nothing for ultimate growth.

So yes, pay attention to Nadabrahma. And sometimes sitting silently, start chanting anything; *aum* will do, or choose anything, any word, and get in tune with it. The meaning is not important: it can be meaningless, it can be meaningful. *Aum* has no meaning. Or you can create your own mantra and chant it. But remember to slip out of it.

Let the body get drunk, let the mind get drunk, let them fall into a deep love affair with each other, and you slip out of it. Don't stay there too long, otherwise you will fall asleep. And if one falls asleep, it is not meditation. Meditation means awareness. So remember!

OSHO NATARAJ MEDITATION

Nataraj is the energy of dance. This is dance as a total meditation, where all inner division disappears and a subtle, relaxed awareness remains.

This meditation is to be done with its specific OSHO Nataraj Meditation music, which indicates and energetically supports the different stages. For further details, see Appendix II.

INSTRUCTIONS
The meditation lasts 65 minutes and has three stages.

FIRST STAGE: 40 MINUTES
With eyes closed, dance as if possessed. Let your unconscious take over completely. Do not control your movements or be a witness to what is happening. Just be totally in the dance.

SECOND STAGE: 20 MINUTES
Keeping your eyes closed, lie down immediately. Be silent and still.

THIRD STAGE: 5 MINUTES
Dance in celebration and enjoy.

All the devices and all the methods I use are just to make you more and more intensely here and now, to help you to forget the past and the future. Any movement of your body or mind can be used as a jumping board: the emphasis is that you jump into the here and now.

Even dancing can be used, but then be just the dancing, not the dancer. The moment the dancer comes in, the dancing is destroyed. The seeker has come in, the time-oriented has come in; now the movement is divided, the dancing has become superficial, and you have gone far away.

When you are dancing, then be *dancing*, do not be the dancer, and the moment comes when you are just the movement, when there is no division. This non-divided consciousness is meditation.

—

Forget the dancer, the center of the ego. Become the dance. That is the meditation. Dance so deeply that you completely forget that you are dancing and begin to feel that you *are* the dance. The division must disappear. Then it becomes a meditation. If there is division, then it is an exercise: good, healthy, but it cannot be said to be spiritual. It is just a simple dance. Dance is good in itself. As far as it goes, it is good. After it, you will feel fresh, young. But it is not yet meditation. The dancer must go, until only the dance remains.

So what to do? – dance so totally, because division can exist only if you are not total in it. If you are standing aside and looking at your own dance, the division will remain: you are the dancer and you are dancing. Then dancing is just an act, something you are doing. It is not your being. Get involved totally, be merged in it. Don't stand aside, don't be an observer – participate!

Let the dance flow in its own way. Don't force it. Rather, follow it. Just follow it: don't force it, allow it to happen. It is not a doing but a happening.

Remain in the mood of festivity. You are not doing something very serious. You're just playing, playing with your life energy, playing with your own bioenergy, allowing your bioenergy to move, to move in its own way. Just as the wind blows and the river flows, you are flowing and blowing. Feel it.

And be playful. Always remember this word *playful*. With me, it is very basic. In this country, we call creation God's *leela*. We call creation God's *leela*, God's play. Nowhere else in the world does this concept exist.

More OSHO Active Meditations
Many more OSHO Active Meditations – including OSHO Devavani Meditation, OSHO Gourishankar Meditation, OSHO Mandala Meditation and others – are spread throughout this book. To find a specific meditation, see Appendix I: Index of Meditations.

9

OSHO TALKS:
SILENCE SHARED IN WORDS

I have to start with your language, and slowly, slowly you will
start learning my language. I am bilingual and I will make you
also bilingual. There are two languages: the language of words
and the language of silence. Right now I have to use
the language of words to translate the poetry of silence, the
music of silence.
Later on, when you have developed a little meditativeness,
you will be able to understand the poetry of silence,
the music of silence directly.

Osho has created many meditation techniques, including his active meditations and meditative therapies. He describes these as effective and direct techniques for the people of today to have a taste of meditation. Uniquely, his talks are also shaped in such a way that they function as a technique to take people into an experience of silence and no-mind. Speaking on the full range of issues relevant for today's humanity – talking to people individually, in small groups, and predominantly to large international audiences – his talks function on many levels. They share a vision, a wealth of techniques for transformation, and a deep experience of silence.

All his public talks have been recorded, early on in audio format and later on video. Osho has used these media throughout his public life to reach people not in his direct presence, while simultaneously making sure that this unique and mystical sharing will continue to be available long beyond his lifetime.

These discourses are the foundations of your meditation. I am crazy, but not so crazy that I should go on speaking four hours a day if it does not help you in meditation! Do you think I am trying to distract you from meditation?

The use of technology
I can be in my room, and I can fill the whole earth with my message. It would be very unintelligent to go on walking from one village to another village. Buddha was helpless. If I had been there in Buddha's time I would have done the same. If Buddha were here now he would do the same.

Man has invented great technology. Everybody else is using that technology, but when it is used for truth, questions start arising. If you use it for business, good; if you use it for politics, good; if you use it for evil, perfectly right, but if you use it for God, then questions start arising.

I am going to use all kinds of media.

—

Not only here where I am speaking, but far away... Anywhere in the world where people will be listening to the video or to the audio, they will come to the same silence.

—

Whatever I am saying is not just for you. It is for all of my sannyasins around the world, my sympathizers, my lovers, and they must be in millions. And it is not even just for them. I am talking also for the future generations.

A video is a far better way to reach people because they can hear me the same way as you are hearing me. Just hearing the words without seeing the person is one thing; seeing the person too makes a lot of difference. It is totally different because when you are listening to me on an audio recording, you will not be able to see my hand, which says more than I can say with my words. You will not be looking at my eyes, which have much more to say than words can convey.

The purpose

My purpose is unique – I am using words just to create silent gaps. The words are not important, so I can say anything contradictory, anything absurd, anything unrelated, because my purpose is just to create gaps. The words are secondary; the silences between those words are primary. This is simply a device to give you a glimpse of meditation. And once you know that it is possible for you, you have traveled far in the direction of your own being.

Most people in the world don't think that it is possible for the mind to be silent. Because they don't think it is possible, they don't try. My basic reason to speak was to give people a taste of meditation, so I can go on speaking eternally – it does not matter what I am saying. All that matters is that I give you a few chances to be silent, which you find difficult on your own in the beginning.

I cannot force you to be silent, but I can create a device in which you are spontaneously bound to be silent. I am speaking, and in the middle of a sentence, when you were expecting another word to follow, nothing follows but a silent gap. And your mind was looking for something to listen to, was waiting for something to follow, and does not want to miss it – naturally it becomes silent. What can the poor mind do? If it was well-known at what points I would be silent, if it was declared to you that at such and such points I would be silent, then you could manage to think – you would not be silent. Then you would know: "This is the point where he is going to be silent, now I can have a little chitchat with myself." But because it comes so suddenly... I don't know myself why at certain points I stop.

Anything like this in any orator in the world will be condemned, because an orator stopping again and again means he is not well prepared, he has not done his homework. It means that his memory is not reliable, that sometimes he cannot find a word to use. But because it is not oratory, I am not concerned about the people who will condemn me – I am concerned with you.

Not only here where I am speaking, but far away... Anywhere in the world where people will be listening to the video or to the audio, they will come to the same silence. My success is not in convincing you, my success is in giving you a real taste so that you can become confident that meditation is not a fiction, that the state of no-mind is not just a philosophical idea, that it is a reality; that you *are* capable of it, and that it does not need any special qualifications.

—

These are not ordinary discourses or talks. I am not interested in any philosophy or any political ideology. I am interested directly in transforming you.

—

I was a teacher of philosophy for nine years, and finding that there was nothing except words, I entered the world of mysticism. There, I have found what was missing in all the philosophies, in all the logical treatises. But now it is impossible to say it. Still I speak. I have been speaking for thirty years continuously – round and round, hoping that somebody may be caught in the net of words and may be pulled out of the misery in which he is drowning. The words can do that much. They can pull you out of your logical world, your linguistic world, your world of philosophies. That too is great. Half the work is done; the remaining can be done by meditation.

—

So if you can feel in my words the sound of silence, my purpose is fulfilled. Because my words are not being used in the same way as words have been used by everybody else. I am using words just as instruments of music. I am not a musician, but I can create the same situation with words and the silences in between. Those who cling to my words miss me because they start interpreting. They start finding contradictions, they start agreeing or disagreeing, but certainly a process of judgment starts in their being. That was not my purpose. My purpose was to start a silence, a music, a fragrance in you.

You have to change the gestalt. From the words and their meaning – which is the ordinary way humanity has used words forever, and nobody has insisted on changing the gestalt – listen to the silences. Read between the lines and you will find a tremendous explosion of silence, music, celebration. And flowers will go on growing in your being.

Why do I go on speaking? Why can't I sit silently here? You will not be able to absorb that much silence. You can absorb it only in homeopathic doses, just once in a while.

And my words help. They don't state the truth, but they help, they indicate; they are fingers pointing to the moon. They are not the moon themselves, just fingers pointing to the moon, arrows. Don't be obsessed by the fingers, don't start clinging to the fingers, don't start worshipping the fingers – because that is how you will miss the moon. Forget the fingers and look at the moon. That moon is silence, utter silence, where not even a single word has ever been uttered.

You have that space inside you. I have become one with it. You are not one with it, but moving with me, flowing with me, hearing my words, listening to my silences, once in a while it happens. And those moments are of grace. In those moments you have the first taste of godliness. Slowly, slowly you will become more and more capable. That's why I go on speaking.

And then, new people are always coming; I have to speak for them. The older ones, slowly, slowly will not be bothered by my words. Hearing will disappear completely. They will listen to my words just as they listen to the sound of a waterfall; they will not search for any meaning in them, they will not search for any truth in them. They will not search even for any coherence in them. They will not be constantly looking into consistency, contradiction, logic, illogic – no, all these things by and by disappear. They will listen to my words as they listen to the songs of the birds, or the wind passing through the pine trees.

You don't ask what the meaning is, you simply listen, and in listening you become that sound passing through the pine trees, you become that wind. Whatsoever I say is a device, so it is a lie. Truth has never been said, cannot be said. Truth is unutterable. But you can listen to it. It is unutterable; it can't be said, but it can be listened to. Let me repeat: it cannot be uttered, but it can be listened to. You can catch hold of it – in silence, in love, in communion. I am not able to say it, but you are able to listen to it; hence, this device of talking to you every morning, year in, year out. This is just a waterfall: listen to it, don't remain just hearing.

How to listen

You are listening to me, you are listening through the ears. You are looking at me, you are looking through the eyes. Certainly you are not the ears and you are not the eyes. The eyes and ears are windows – somebody is hidden behind, standing behind the windows.

Just watch – your eyes are windows. When you are looking at me you are looking through the eyes. But who are you? Who is it who is looking at me? Who is it who is hearing? What is this consciousness?

You are not to agree or disagree because if you start agreeing or disagreeing, you miss the point.

Listen silently as if you are listening to the sound of a river, or the sound of the wind blowing through the pine trees. Just hear it, without bringing your mind in to say "Yes, it is right" or "No, it is not right."

Any statement or interpretation by your mind is going to distort the whole thing. The statement is not linguistic. It is not the language; it is something invisible, side by side with the language, that is being transmitted. So if you silently hear, the language does not matter. Your silence grows deeper – that's what matters. What the language was saying is immaterial, it was just a vehicle.

You are listening: you can listen in the right way, you can listen in the wrong way.

If you are listening with all kinds of prejudices, that is a wrong way of listening; it is really a way of not listening. You appear to be listening, but you are only hearing, not listening. Right listening means you have put aside your mind. It does not mean that you become gullible, that you start believing whatsoever is said to you. It has nothing to do with belief or disbelief. Right listening means, "I am not concerned right now whether to believe or not to believe. There is no question of agreement or disagreement at this moment. I am simply trying to listen to whatsoever it is. Later on I can decide what is right and what is wrong. Later on I can decide whether to follow or not to follow."

The beauty of right listening is that truth has a music of its own. If you can listen without prejudice, your heart will say it is true. If it is true, a bell starts ringing in your heart. If it is not true, you remain aloof, unconcerned, indifferent; no bell rings in your heart, no synchronicity happens. That is the quality of truth: if you listen to it with an open heart, it immediately creates a response in your being – your very center is uplifted. You start growing wings; suddenly the whole sky is open.

It is not a question of deciding logically whether what is being said is true or untrue. On the contrary, it is a question of love, not of logic. Truth immediately creates a love in your heart; something is triggered in you in a very mysterious way.

But if you listen wrongly – that is, full of your mind, full of your garbage, full of your knowledge – then you will not allow your heart to respond to the truth. You will miss the tremendous possibility, you will miss the synchronicity. Your heart was ready to respond to truth. It responds only to truth, remember, it never responds to the untrue. With the untrue it remains utterly silent, unresponsive, unaffected, unstirred. With the truth it starts dancing, it starts singing, as if suddenly the sun has risen and the dark night is no more, and the birds are singing and the lotuses opening, and the whole earth is awakened.

Thousands of Osho's extemporaneous talks, known as OSHO Talks, are available in multiple media formats. For further details, see Appendix II.

10

OSHO EVENING MEETING MEDITATION

This is a great event; each evening you go a little deeper into your buddhahood. Look around this empty space within you. You have to remember it, twenty-four hours, when you come back from the inner journey.

As mentioned in the previous chapter "OSHO Talks: Silence Shared in Words," the essence of Osho's Talks is that they function as a meditation for his audience – both the audience in his physical presence and the audience spread all over the world; and both during and after his lifetime.

Osho's daily talks have culminated in his creating and refining the expanded "Evening Meeting Meditation" described in this chapter. The meditation has many aspects which perhaps can only be described as "mystical." One of the mysteries is Osho calling it a "meeting." It is intended for anyone exploring Osho's approach and methods, to be done at 7:00 PM local time. As the globe turns, the meditation will always be in progress somewhere. No matter who, no matter where, no matter whether alone or together with others, it is an on-going chain of meditation that everyone interested can participate in, in perpetuity.

The unique importance of the meditation is indicated by Osho's request that all other programs in his Meditation Resort and in the OSHO centers worldwide be stopped completely while it is in progress, and for everyone to attend.

This meditation is done with:
1. *its specific OSHO Evening Meeting Meditation music, which indicates and energetically supports particular stages*
2. *an OSHO Talk*
3. *a Gibberish and Let-go recording*
For further details, see Appendix II.

INSTRUCTIONS

The duration of the Evening Meeting Meditation varies according to the length of the chosen OSHO talk. The first stage of dancing and celebration is to be completed at precisely 7:00 PM.

When done in its full format*, these are the steps:

1.	DANCING CELEBRATION	10-20 MINUTES, ENDING AT 7:00 PM
2.	INDIAN CLASSICAL MUSIC AND SILENCE	10 MINUTES
3.	OSHO TALK	40 MINUTES OR LONGER
4.	GIBBERISH, SILENCE & LET-GO	10-15 MINUTES
5.	CELEBRATION	2-5 MINUTES

1. DANCING CELEBRATION

The meditation starts with high-energy music for dancing and celebrating with totality – a wild celebration, raising the energy and building it to a peak, with as much delight as possible. You can keep your eyes open or closed; remain just with yourself. The dancing includes three or four "stops": sharp shouts of the sound "OSHO" while your arms reach straight "up to the stars, indicating the longing for higher consciousness."

Osho calls the sound of "OSHO" "a good sound," saying "It creates a good silence. It is not my name. It is only a healing sound." And about making the shout: "It goes just like a sword. It all depends with how much intensity, urgency, totality, you do it. It is simply using sound to reach the soundless silence." "You can say it in a lukewarm way – then you will miss it. It has to be said exactly like the lion's roar, which comes from the belly. It is not just from your tongue – not even from your throat or your heart. It hits exactly just below the navel – two inches below to be exact. You should watch. Whenever you do it, you should keep an eye on where it is coming from – that is the way for you to go in. It is clearing the way, it is making a passage in a forgotten land, giving you a direct line. It connects you with yourself."

The more total your participation is in this buildup of energy, the deeper your silence will be in the next part of the meditation. The celebration reaches its peak at 7:00 PM with three consecutive shouts of the sound "OSHO."

2. INDIAN CLASSICAL MUSIC AND SILENCE

Immediately after the 7:00 PM peak of celebration with three consecutive shouts of OSHO, sit down in pin-drop silence, eyes closed. Ten minutes of Indian music, alternating with sudden stops, follows. This stage ends with three explosive drumbeats.

3. OSHO TALK

Continue to sit silently, eyes open or closed, during an OSHO Talk on audio or video. (Chapter 9, OSHO Talks: Silence Shared in Words, contains more information on this part of the meditation.)

I don't speak to teach something; I speak to create something. These are not lectures. These are simply devices for you to become silent because if you are told to become silent without making any effort, you will find great difficulty.

That's what Zen teachers have been telling their disciples: "Be silent, but don't make any effort." Now, you are putting the person into such a difficult fix: "Don't make any effort and be silent." Now, if he makes any effort he is wrong – and there is no way to be silent without making an effort. If it were possible to be silent without any effort there would have been no need of any master, there would have been no need to teach meditation. People would have become silent without any effort.

I have gone as deep as possible into Zen efforts. They have been working for almost fourteen centuries, since Bodhidharma. They are one of the greatest groups in the world, totally devoted to a single thing and that is meditation. There is no other experiment anywhere that has been done for so long continuously. But still there are not many Zen masters.

Yes, there are more masters in the stream of Zen than in any other stream in the world, but still they are very few compared to the people who have been working. I have been searching for what was the basic mistake. This is the basic mistake: those Zen masters told them the right thing but not in the right way. I am making you aware of silences without any effort on your part. My speaking is being used for the first time as a strategy to create silence in you.

—

When you see me, you are seeing me; your consciousness is single-arrowed – arrowed toward me. If you change... You can do this right now, and it will be good to do it, to understand that you are looking at me; how your eyes are arrowed at me. If you are really arrowed at me, you will forget yourself. This is forgetfulness. Now make your consciousness double-arrowed. Look at me and at the same time, simultaneously, look at yourself. Look at the looked-at, and then look at the looker-on – the viewed and the viewer.

When you are listening to me, listen, and always become aware of the listener too. The speaker must be listened to, and the listener must be listened to also. Then your consciousness has double arrows. Right now it is one-way traffic: you look at me and you are not looking at yourself. This is a sort of self-forgetfulness.

If you look at me and simultaneously become capable of looking at yourself, in that moment self-awareness happens. Buddha calls it *samyak smriti*; Kabir calls it *surati*; Gurdjieff calls it self-remembering. But it is the same.

The art of listening is based on silencing the mind, so that the mind does not interfere, it simply allows whatever is coming to you. I am not saying you have to agree with it. Listening does not mean that you have to agree with it, neither does it mean that you have to disagree with it. The art of listening is just pure listening, factual, undistorted. And once you have listened, then comes the point whether you agree or not, but the first thing is to listen.

If you listen to something that is true, there is no question of disagreement. If it is untrue, naturally you have to disagree with it. But your agreement or disagreement should come not from the prejudiced mind, but from the unprejudiced heart. Listening is from the heart, and hearing is from the mind, it is very superficial. And because the heart is deeper, any word that enters you first has to encounter the mind. Before it reaches the heart, the mind has done many things with it.

And if you are capable of listening there is nothing left for you to do. In that silence you will be able to see without any argumentation within you what is right and what is not right. The right immediately makes you so joyful and the wrong immediately makes you sad and aloof. It is a totally different kind of differentiation than mental talk: "This is right; this is wrong." On what grounds can your mind say, "This is right"? It is your prejudice; it is your preconceived idea.

But the heart has no preconceived ideas. It simply sees clearly. It has eyes but no ideas. It has clarity but no prejudices.

Shravan means listening, and *shravaka* means the listener, one who is capable of listening in the sense I have defined listening; one who need not do anything else, just listening will be enough.

The art of listening is the simplest method of transformation.

At the end of the talk Osho creates a few moments of laughter, before moving to the next stage of the meditation:

4. GIBBERISH, SILENCE & LET-GO
This short meditation has the following steps:

A. Gibberish
B. Freeze, no movement, go in
C. Let-go
D. Come back to life

Gibberish is to get rid of the active mind, silence to get rid of the inactive mind, and the let-go to enter into the transcendental. Each step starts with a drumbeat.

A. Gibberish
This first step starts with a drumbeat. You remain sitting and for a few minutes you go completely mad, saying anything that is moving in your mind, all kinds of rubbish – throw it out, speaking in any language you don't know! Be total. It is one of the most scientific ways to clean your mind. Here are some of the points Osho makes about gibberish:

- With the first drumbeat, start throwing out as much rubbish as possible, with gibberish and gestures. It is a cleansing, a preparation for silence.
- Don't say things which are meaningful, don't use the language that you know. Use Chinese, if you don't know Chinese. Use Japanese, if you don't know Japanese. Don't use German if you know German. For the first time have a freedom the same as all the birds have. Simply allow whatever comes to your mind without bothering about its rationality, reason-ability, meaning, significance – just the way the birds are doing.
- Say everything that you ever wanted to say and have not been able to say because of civilization, education, culture, society.
- Gibberish simply means throwing out your craziness that is already there in the mind, piled up for centuries. As you throw it out you will find yourself becoming light, becoming more alive, just within two minutes.
- Be total because once you are freed of it, there is a possibility

of going deeper into silence than you have ever gone.
- The more you put into it, the deeper will be the following silence. So don't be partial, don't be middle-class. Just be a first-rate crazy man!
- It has been roaming inside you: allow it freedom.
- And as the mind becomes silent, there is nowhere to go other than inward. All roads are forgotten, there remains a single one-way traffic.
- It will make you saner than you have ever been because you throw out so much garbage that you were holding.

(See also the "OSHO No-Mind" section in chapter 11: OSHO Meditative Therapies.)

B. *Freeze, no movement, go in*
The two minutes of gibberish have cleaned the way for entering into silence as deeply as you have never done before. Now close your eyes and freeze your body, all its movements – gathering your energy within and remaining here and now. "Once you are out of the mind, you are in. To be in the mind is to be out of yourself. To be out of the mind is to be in your own being."
During this part of the meditation, using words and silent gaps, Osho encourages you to move inward...

Be silent. Close your eyes. Feel your body to be completely frozen.

Now, look inward with your total consciousness, and with an urgency as if this is your last moment of life.

Your center of being is not far away. All that you need is just a total urgency.

Deeper and deeper, like a spear... The deeper you go into your being, the deeper you are going into existence.

This moment you are a buddha, and to be a buddha is to attain to the ultimate potential of your being. The seed comes to blossom in a blue lotus.

This very body the buddha, this very earth the lotus paradise.

Remain a witness. That is the only thing that is eternal in you. Everything is mortal except witnessing. Witnessing is another name of the buddha.

C. Let-go

With the next drumbeat you let go, allowing your body to fall like a bag of rice or like a falling tree, to "die" – lying utterly still and relaxed.
Using words and silent gaps, Osho's voice encourages you to continue moving inward...

Relax. But remain alert; a witness of your body, of your mind, and all that is happening in this moment within you.
The silence, the peace, the bliss...
As you go deeper, the splendor becomes richer and richer. As you go deeper, life becomes a mystery, a miracle of immense significance. And a deep gratitude arises, just for all that existence has done for you. It is not a prayer, it is a thankfulness.

The evening was beautiful on its own, but your witnessing, your consciousness, has added thousands of stars to its beauty. Gather as much of the experience as you can, because you have to bring it to the circumference, to your actual life. It has to become a twenty-four-hour, round-the-clock experience. Slowly, slowly the circumference and the center come closer. One day the circumference disappears into the center: you have attained perfect buddhahood.

D. Come back to life

You are invited to come back to a sitting position, with the reminder to carry this same experience of witnessing into all your activities, twenty-four hours a day...

Come back, but now come a little more alert, a little more of a buddha, a little more loving, a little more graceful. Sit down for a few moments, just to recollect the path you have gone in, and the path that you have come out. It is the same path, the golden path.

You have to live your experience in your life, in your activities, in your gestures, in your relations with people. Remember you are a buddha and you have to behave like a buddha, and you will find great transforming forces entering your life. The whole existence becomes supportive – supportive of your metamorphosis.

5. CELEBRATION

The Evening Meeting Meditation concludes with dancing in celebration, eyes open or closed.

It is not without a reason that I want you to end your meditation every day with celebration, with rejoicing. Slowly, slowly, as meditation becomes deeper, your celebration will have more splendor; it will be more majestic, more miraculous, more magical.

* A starter version of the OSHO Evening Meeting Meditation, for live participation, is available on http://imeditate.osho.com.

11

OSHO MEDITATIVE THERAPIES

I am giving you a very fundamental technique, fresh and
unused. And it is going to become worldwide, without any
doubt, because its effects will show anybody that the person
has become younger, the person has become more loving,
the person has become graceful.
The person has become more flexible, less fanatic;
the person has become more joyful, more a celebrant.
All that this world needs is a good cleansing of the heart
of all the inhibitions of the past.

*Created by Osho, the first three OSHO Meditative Therapies are
radical expressive processes that lead to a final stage of silent
self-awareness.*

*Uniquely simple and effective, these energetic methods involve a
minimum of interaction among the participants, but the energy of the
group and the presence of a trained facilitator help each individual
go more deeply into his or her own process.*

*The fourth is a guided process for activating the self-healing powers
of the bodymind and for making friends with oneself.*

*OSHO Meditative Therapies are offered regularly at the OSHO
International Meditation Resort in Pune, India, and at larger OSHO
Meditation Centers worldwide. Once you have participated in the
group process, you can continue the method alone at home whenever you like.*

OSHO MYSTIC ROSE

*This is a three-week process, lasting three hours per day. During the
first week you laugh, for no reason at all, dissolving the layers of
dust, inhibitions, and repressions that prevent inner spontaneity and
joy. The second week is devoted to weeping and crying for no reason at all – allowing the pain and the tears that are ready to come
and which we have been preventing. The third week is for silence and
stillness – the watcher on the hills – silent watching, meditation.*

The symbol of the mystic rose is that, if man takes care of
the seed that he is born with, gives it the right soil, gives it the
right atmosphere and the right vibrations, moves on a right path
where the seed can start growing, then the ultimate growth is
symbolized as the mystic rose – when your being blossoms and
opens all its petals and releases a beautiful fragrance.

The first part will be "Yaa-Hoo!" For three hours, people
simply laugh for no reason at all, and whenever their laughter
starts dying they again say, "Yaa-Hoo!" and it will come back.
Digging for three hours, you will be surprised how many layers of dust have gathered upon your being. It will cut them like
a sword, in one blow. For seven days continuously, three hours

every day... You cannot conceive how much transformation can come to your being.

Then the second part is "Yaa-Boo." The first part removes everything that hinders your laughter – all the inhibitions of past humanity, all the repressions. It cuts them away. It brings a new space within you, but still you have to go a few steps more to reach the temple of your being because you have suppressed so much sadness, so much despair, so much anxiety, so many tears. They are all there, covering you and destroying your beauty, your grace, your joy.

If you go in, you will find both laughter and tears. That's why sometimes it happens that by laughing, suddenly you find tears also start coming together with the laughter. It is confusing because ordinarily we think they are contrary. When you are full of tears it is not a time to laugh, or when you are laughing it is not the right season for tears. But existence does not believe in your concepts, ideologies; existence transcends all your concepts, which are dualistic, which are based on duality. Day and night, laughter and tears, pain and blissfulness, they both come together.

When a man reaches his innermost being he will find the first layer is of laughter and the second layer is of agony, tears.

So for seven days you have to allow yourself to weep, cry, for no reason at all – the tears are ready to come. It is just that you have been preventing them. Just don't prevent, and whenever you feel they are not coming, just say, "Yaa-Boo!"

These are pure sounds, used as a technique to bring all your laughter and all your tears and clean you completely, so that you can become an innocent child.

This is absolutely my meditation.

—

You will be surprised that no meditation can give you as much as this small strategy can. This is my experience of many meditations, that what has to be done is to break these two layers in you. Your laughter has been repressed; you have been told, "Don't laugh, it is a serious matter." You are not allowed to laugh in a church, or in a university class.

So the first layer is of laughter, but once laughter is over you will suddenly find yourself flooded with tears, agony. But that too will be a great unburdening phenomenon. Many lives of pain and suffering will disappear. If you can get rid of these two layers you have found yourself.

There is no meaning in the words, *Yaa-Hoo* or *Yaa-Boo*. These are simply techniques, sounds which can be used for a certain purpose, to enter your own being.

You may have felt it when you shout, "Yaa-Hoo!" You may have felt a sudden breeze of freshness and joy.

I have invented many meditations, but perhaps this will be the most essential and fundamental one. It can take over the whole world.

Every society has done so much harm by preventing your joys and your tears. If an old man starts crying you will say, "What are you doing? You should feel ashamed; you are not a child, it is not that somebody has taken your banana and you are crying. Have another banana, but don't cry."

Just see – stand on the street and start crying and a crowd will gather to console you: "Don't cry! Whatever has happened, forget all about it, it has happened." Nobody knows what has happened, nobody can help you, but everybody will try – "Don't cry!" And the reason is that if you go on crying, then they will start crying because they are also flooded with tears.

Those tears are very close to the eyes. It is a healthy thing to cry, to weep, to laugh. Now scientists are discovering that crying, weeping, laughter, are immensely healthful; not only physically but also psychologically, they are very capable of keeping you sane. The whole of humanity has gone a little cuckoo, for the simple reason that nobody laughs fully because all around there are people who will say, "What are you doing? Are you a child? At this age? What will your children think? Keep quiet!"

If you cry and weep without any reason, just as an exercise, a meditation, nobody will believe it. Tears have never been accepted as a meditation. And I tell you, they are not only a meditation, they are a medicine also. You will have better eyesight and you will have better inner vision.

I am giving you a very fundamental technique, fresh and unused. And it is going to become worldwide, without any doubt, because its effects will show anybody that the person has become younger, the person has become more loving, the person has become graceful. The person has become more flexible, less fanatic; the person has become more joyful, more a celebrant.

All that this world needs is a good cleansing of the heart of all the inhibitions of the past. Laughter and tears can do both. Tears will take out all the agony that is hidden inside you and laughter will take all that is preventing your ecstasy. Once you have learned the art you will be immensely surprised: Why has this not been told up to now? There is a reason: nobody has wanted humanity to have the freshness of a roseflower and the fragrance and the beauty.

The third step is silence. I have called it "The Watcher on the Hills." Become as silent as if you are alone on the top of a Himalayan peak – utterly silent and alone, just watching, listening... Sensitive, but still.

OSHO NO-MIND

This is a one-week process, lasting two hours per day.
The first hour is for gibberish: going consciously crazy, allowing any
sounds which come from inside, in any language except a language
you know – emptying the mind of all garbage. The second hour is
for sitting silently, doing nothing – allowing a great silence to arise
from within.

The first part is gibberish. The word *gibberish* comes from a
Sufi mystic, Jabbar. Jabbar never spoke any language, he just
uttered nonsense. Still, he had thousands of disciples because
what he was saying was, "Your mind is nothing but gibberish.
Put it aside and you will have a taste of your own being."

Gibberish means, don't say things which are meaningful, don't use the language that you know. Use Chinese, if you
don't know Chinese. Use Japanese, if you don't know Japanese.
Don't use German if you know German. For the first time have
a freedom the same as all the birds have. Simply allow whatever comes to your mind without bothering about its rationality, reasonability, meaning, significance – just the way the birds
are doing.

For the first part, leave language, mind aside.

Out of this will arise the second part, a great silence in which
you have to close your eyes and freeze your body, all its movements, gather your energy within yourself, remain here and now.
Zen cannot be understood in any other way.

OSHO BORN AGAIN

This is a one-week process, lasting two hours per day.
For the first hour you behave like a child, just enter your childhood.
Whatever you wanted to do, do it – dancing, singing, jumping, crying, weeping – anything at all, in any posture. Nothing is prohibited except touching other people. Don't touch or harm anyone else in the group.
For the second hour just sit silently. You will be fresher, more innocent, and meditation will become easier.

This great experiment through which you are passing is basically to achieve your lost childhood again.

When I say "your lost childhood," I mean your innocence, your eyes full of wonder, knowing nothing, having nothing, but yet feeling yourself at the top of the world. Those golden moments of wonder, joy, no tension, no worry, no anxiety, have to be regained, rediscovered. The sage is nothing but the circle that started in your birth coming all the way, complete, back to the same point.

OSHO REMINDING YOURSELF OF THE FORGOTTEN LANGUAGE OF TALKING TO YOUR BODYMIND

This is a guided one-week process, lasting one hour per day. It can then be continued or refreshed at any time.

The method is based on the understanding that we need to be taught anew to create friendship with our bodies and minds; these are not separate from us or from one another. We need to remember "the forgotten language" of communicating with the bodymind about those areas where our tensions and pains exist.

In a light trance, while combining deep relaxation with alertness, you learn to harness the bodymind's creative and self-healing energies. These can be brought to any specific issues of imbalance or unease, such as smoking, eating imbalances, insomnia, aches and pain – any functions that are normally part of the body and which need to be brought to wholeness and balance again.

The seven-day process is offered at the OSHO International Meditation Resort in Pune, India, and in a number of OSHO centers.
The method is also available in many languages as a one-hour guided process, accompanied by its specific music which energetically supports the different stages. For further details, see Appendix II.

You cannot torture the body and raise your consciousness. The body has to be loved – you have to be a great friend. It is your home, you have to clean it of all junk, and you have to remember that it is in your service continuously, day in, day out. Even when you are asleep, your body is continuously working for you, digesting, changing your food into blood, taking out the dead cells from the body, bringing new oxygen, fresh oxygen into the body – and you are fast asleep!

It is doing everything for your survival, for your life, although you are so ungrateful that you have never even thanked your body. On the contrary, your religions have been teaching you to torture it: the body is your enemy and you have to get free from the body, its attachments. I also know that you are more than the body and there is no need to have any attachment. But love is not an attachment, compassion is not an attachment. Love and compassion are absolutely needed for your body and its nourish-ment. And the better body you have, the more are the possibilities for growing consciousness. It is an organic unity.

⁓

The first step in relaxing is the body. Remember as many times as possible to look into the body, whether you are carry-ing some tension in the body somewhere – at the neck, in the head, in the legs. Relax it consciously. Just go to that part of the body and persuade that part, say to it lovingly "Relax."

And you will be surprised that if you approach any part of your body, it listens, it follows you – it is your body! With closed eyes, go inside the body from the toe to the head searching for any place where there is a tension. And then talk to that part as you talk to a friend; let there be a dialogue between you and your body. Tell it to relax, and tell it, "There is nothing to fear. Don't be afraid. I am here to take care – you can relax." Slowly, slowly you will learn the knack of it. Then the body becomes relaxed.

Then take another step, a little deeper: tell the mind to relax. And if the body listens, the mind also listens, but you cannot start with the mind – you have to start from the beginning. You cannot start from the middle. Many people start with the mind and they fail; they fail because they start from a wrong place. Everything should be done in the right order.

If you become capable of relaxing the body voluntarily, then you will be able to help your mind relax voluntarily. Mind is a more complex phenomenon.

⁓

Your mind and your body are not two things...

Remember that always. Do not say, "physiological process" and "mental process." They are not two – just two parts of one whole. Whatsoever you do physiologically affects the mind. Whatsoever you do psychologically affects the body. They are not two, they are one.

You can say that the body is the solid state of an energy and the mind is the liquid state of the same energy – of the same energy! So whatever you are doing physiologically, do not think that it is just physiological: How it is going to help any transformation in the mind? If you take alcohol, what happens to your mind? Alcohol is taken in the body, not in the mind, and what happens to the mind? If you take LSD, it goes into the body, not into the mind, and what happens to the mind?

Or if you go on a fast, fasting is done by the body, and what happens to the mind? Or from the other end: if you think sexual thoughts, what happens to your body? The body is affected immediately. You think in the mind of a sex object and your body starts getting ready.

Physiological processes and psychological processes are not two things, they are one, and you can start from either to affect and change the other.

12

BREATH MEDITATIONS

If you can do something with the breath,
you will suddenly turn to the present.
If you can do something with breath,
you will attain the source of life.
If you can do something with breath,
you can transcend time and space.
If you do something with breath,
you will be in the world and also beyond it.

OSHO VIPASSANA MEDITATION

This method is based on a method of Gautama the Buddha. It is for practicing awareness, watchfulness, mindfulness, witnessing. The OSHO form of vipassana enables this to be a comfortable, "juicy" experience, it is not dry.
Vipassana can be done in different ways. Following is a one-hour OSHO format, divided into two stages.

INSTRUCTIONS
The meditation lasts one hour and has two stages. You will be sitting for 45 minutes followed by 15 minutes of slow walking meditation. You may also choose to continue sitting for the whole hour.

FIRST STAGE: 45 MINUTES
Find a comfortable sitting position. It is fine to change your position if you need to, moving slowly, with awareness. While sitting your eyes are closed.
The essence of vipassana is to watch and accept whatever is happening. While sitting, the primary object to be watching is the rise and fall of the belly, slightly above the navel, caused by natural breathing. It is not a concentration technique, so while watching the breath, many other things will take your attention away. Nothing is a disturbance in vipassana, it includes everything such as thoughts, judgments, feelings, body sensations and impressions from the outside world. Watch whatever comes up and gently return to the breath when you have the choice. Remember that it is the process of watching that is important, not so much what you are watching.

SECOND STAGE: 15 MINUTES
Now the primary object to be watching is the sensation of the feet touching the ground while walking. Your attention may go onto other things. Notice what arises and whenever you have the choice, gently bring your attention back to the feet touching the ground.
Keep your eyes lowered, looking a few steps ahead. It is a slow natural walk, about half your normal speed.

Note: If you are doing this in a group setting with a facilitator present, then while sitting you may be tapped on the head with the vipassana stick. This is to help you to be alert and give you extra energy and encouragement for watching.

Here, vipassana is a juicy experience; it is not dry.

I have a few criticisms against the vipassana that is being practiced in Buddhist lands. They have all made it very dry, desert-like; nothing blossoms, no greenery; everything is simply businesslike. I want you to learn meditation as a play, as playfulness. Your meditation and your love should be synonymous.

Life is accepted in its totality. In this total acceptance arises the awareness that will enable you to meditate. And this meditation will be far richer than any vipassana of Gautam Buddha. This meditation may create songs in you, may create dances in you, may give a new impetus toward creativity in all dimensions of life.

Your silence should not be the silence of a graveyard, your silence should be the silence of a garden. Once in a while a bird starts singing, but it does not disturb the silence, it deepens it. Once in a while the breeze comes with its song, passes through the pine trees, but it does not disturb the silence, it deepens it.

I do not teach you the desert. I teach you the garden, the garden of the heart. That is where, with great respect, I differ from Gautam Buddha. I love the man, but that does not mean I have to agree with everything done by him. His meditation is heartless, and a meditation that is heartless is not of any worth. I want a meditation that can laugh, that can dance.

—

Vipassana is the meditation that has made more people in the world enlightened than any other because it is the very essence. All other meditations have the same essence, but in different forms; something nonessential is also joined with them. But vipassana is pure essence. You cannot drop anything out of it and you cannot add anything to improve it.

Vipassana is such a simple thing that even a small child can do it. In fact, the smallest child can do it better than you because he is not yet filled with the garbage of the mind; he is still clean and innocent.

Vipassana can be done in three ways – you can choose which one suits you the best.

The first is: awareness of your actions, your body, your mind, your heart. Walking, you should walk with awareness. Moving your hand, you should move with awareness, knowing perfectly that you are moving the hand. You can move it without any consciousness, like a mechanical thing... You are on a morning walk; you can go on walking without being aware of your feet.

Be alert of the movements of your body. While eating, be alert to the movements that are needed for eating. Taking a shower, be alert to the coolness that is coming to you, the water falling on you and the tremendous joy of it – just be alert. It should not go on happening in an unconscious state.

And the same with your mind. Whatever thought passes on the screen of your mind, just be a watcher. Whatever emotion passes on the screen of your heart, just remain a witness – don't get involved, don't get identified, don't evaluate what is good, what is bad; that is not part of your meditation, your meditation has to be choiceless awareness.

The second form is breathing, becoming aware of breathing. As the breath goes in, your belly starts rising up, and as the breath goes out, your belly starts settling down again. So the second method is to be aware of the belly: its rising and falling. Just the very awareness of the belly rising and falling... And the belly is very close to the life sources because the child is joined with the mother's life through the navel. Behind the navel is his life's source. So, when the belly rises up, it is really the life energy, the spring of life that is rising up and falling down with each breath. That too is not difficult, and perhaps may be easier because it is a single technique.

In the first, you have to be aware of the body, you have to be aware of the mind, you have to be aware of your emotions, moods. So it has three steps. The second approach has a single step: just the belly, moving up and down. And the result is the same. As you become more aware of the belly, the mind becomes silent, the heart becomes silent, the moods disappear.

And the third is to be aware of the breath at the entrance, when the breath goes in through your nostrils. Feel it at that extreme – the other polarity from the belly – feel it at the nose.

The breath going in gives a certain coolness to your nostrils. Then the breath going out... Breath going in, breath going out... These are the three forms. Any one will do. And if you want to do two forms together, you can do two forms together; then the effort will become more intense. If you want to do all three forms together, you can do all three forms together. Then the process will be quicker. But it all depends on you, whatever feels easy.

Remember: easy is right.

WATCHING THE GAP IN THE BREATH

Shiva says: *"Radiant one, this experience may dawn between two breaths. After breath comes in, down, and just before turning up, out, the beneficence."*

After breath comes in – that is, down – *and just before turning out* – that is, going up – *the beneficence.* Be aware between these two points, and the happening. When your breath comes in, observe. When your breath comes in, observe. For a single moment, or a thousandth part of a moment, there is no breathing – before it turns up, before it turns outward. One breath comes in; then there is a certain point when breathing stops. Then the breathing goes out. When the breath goes out, then again for a single moment, or a part of a moment, breathing stops. Then breathing comes in.

Before the turning in or turning out, there is a moment when you are not breathing. In that moment the happening is possible, because when you are not breathing you are not in the world. Understand this: when you are not breathing you are dead; you still *are*, but dead. But the moment is of such a short duration that you never observe it.

Each outgoing breath is a death and each new breath is a rebirth. Breath coming in is rebirth; breath going out is death. The outgoing breath is synonymous with death; the incoming breath is synonymous with life. So with each breath you are dying and being reborn. The gap between the two is of a very short duration, but keen, sincere observation and attention will make you feel the gap.

If you can feel the gap, Shiva says: ...*the beneficence.* Then nothing else is needed. You are blessed, you have known; the thing has happened.

You are not to train the breath. Leave it just as it is. Why such a simple technique? It looks so simple. Such a simple technique to know the truth? To know the truth means to know that which is neither born nor dies, to know that eternal element which is always. You can know the breath going out, you can know the breath coming in, but you never know the gap between the two.

Try it. Suddenly, if you can get the point... And you can get it; it is already there. Nothing is to be added to you or to your structure, it is already there. Everything is already there, only a certain awareness is needed. So, how to do this? First, become aware of the breath coming in. Watch it. Forget everything, just watch the breath coming in – the very passage.

When the breath touches your nostrils, feel it there. Then let the breath move in. Move with the breath fully consciously. You are going down, down, down with the breath, don't miss the breath. Don't go ahead and don't follow behind, just go with it. Remember this: don't go ahead, don't follow it like a shadow; be simultaneous with it.

Breath and consciousness should become one. The breath goes in – you go in. Only then will it be possible to get the point which is between two breaths.

WATCHING THE GAP WHILE IN THE MARKETPLACE

Note: First read the preceding meditation, Watching the Gap in the Breath.

We have discussed one technique that is similar. Now there is only this one difference: that it has to be practiced while in worldly activity. Don't practice it in isolation; just practice it while you are doing something else. You are eating – go on eating and be attentive of the gap. You are walking – go on walking and be attentive of the gap. You are going to sleep – lie down, let sleep come, and go on being attentive of the gap.

Why in activity? – because activity distracts the mind, activity calls for your attention again and again. Don't be distracted, be fixed at the gap. And don't stop activity, let the activity continue. You will have two layers of existence – doing and being.

BREATHING FROM THE SOLES OF YOUR FEET

The lower part of the body is one of the problems for many people – almost the majority. The lower part has gone dead because sex has been repressed through the centuries. People have become afraid to move below the sex center. They just remain uptight, they remain above the sex center. In fact many people live in their heads, or if they are a little more courageous, they live in the torso.

At the most, people go down to the navel but not beyond that, so half of the body is almost paralyzed and because of it, half of life is also paralyzed. Then many things become impossible because the lower part of the body is like the roots. These are the roots. The legs are the roots and they connect you with the earth. So people are hanging like ghosts, unconnected with the earth. One has to move back to the feet.

Lao Tzu used to say to his disciples, "Unless you start breathing from the soles of your feet, you are not my disciples." Breathing from the soles of your feet... He is perfectly right. The deeper you go, the deeper goes your breath. It is almost true that the boundary of your being is the boundary of your breath. When the boundary increases and touches your feet, your breath almost reaches to the feet; not in a physiological sense, but in a very, very psychological sense. Then you have claimed your whole body. For the first time you are whole, one piece, together. So continue to do that exercise.

TWENTY-ONE-DAY EXPERIMENT IN SECLUSION AND SILENCE

Before deciding to do an intensive process like this one, it is good to have had prior experience of OSHO Active Meditations, and also of sitting silently, doing nothing. It is imperative to practice an OSHO Active Meditation, preferably OSHO Dynamic, every day during your experiment in seclusion and silence. The text below is an excerpt. For the full description, see Meditation: The Art of Ecstasy, *#18.*

It is helpful to practice breath awareness for twenty-one days in total seclusion and silence. Then, much will happen.

During the twenty-one-day experiment, practice Dynamic Meditation once a day and constant awareness of breathing for twenty-four hours a day. Do not read, do not write, do not think, because all these acts are of the mental body; they are not concerned with the etheric body.

You can go for a walk. This helps because walking is part of the etheric body; all manual actions are concerned with the prana *sharira*, the etheric body. The physical body does these things, but it is for the etheric body. Everything concerned with the etheric body should be done, and everything concerned with any other body must not be done. You can also have a bath once or twice a day; it is concerned with the etheric body.

When you go for a walk, just walk. Do not do anything else; just be concerned with your walking. And while walking, keep your eyes half-closed. Half-closed eyes cannot see anything other than the path, and the path itself is so monotonous that it will not give you something new to think about.

You must remain in a monotonous world, just in one room, seeing the same floor. It must be so monotonous that you cannot think about it. Thinking needs stimuli; thinking needs new sensations. If your sensory system is constantly bored, there will be nothing outside of you to think about.

As you continue to watch your breath, the breath will become more and more subtle. But awareness, too, will become more subtle because you will be continuing to watch this subtle breath. And when there is no breath, you will be aware of this "no breathness," you will be aware of this harmony; then awareness will penetrate even more deeply. The more subtle the breath is, the more aware you will have to become so that you can be aware of it.

Go on being aware and if you feel that there is no breath,

then be aware of your "no breath." Do not try to breathe; just be aware of "no breathness." This will be a very blissful moment.

If you go on watching your breath and being indifferent to everything that is happening, then the third week will be a week of complete nothingness. It will be as if everything has died, as if everything has gone into nonexistence, and only nothingness remains.

Do not stop the experiment before the twenty-one days are over. After the first week, you may want to stop it. Your mind may say, "This is nonsense. Leave." Do not listen to it. Just tell yourself once and for all that for twenty-one days there is nowhere else to go.

After the third week you may not want to leave. If your mind is so blissful that you do not want to disturb it, if only nothingness, blissfulness is there – if you are just a vacuum – then you can prolong the experiment for two or three or four more days. But do not break it before the twenty-one days are over.

This experiment in seclusion is available on request through the OSHO Multiversity's Living In program at the OSHO International Meditation Resort in Pune, India. You can also decide to do this anywhere else, and arrange for the practicalities such as food and laundry yourself.

13

CHAKRA MEDITATIONS

One has to feel the chakras, not know about them. You have
to feel; you have to send feelers inside yourself.
Only when you feel your chakras, and your kundalini and its
passage, is it helpful; otherwise, it is not helpful.
In fact, knowledge has been very destructive
as far as the inner world is concerned.
The more knowledge gained the less possibility of feeling
the real, the authentic, things.

OSHO CHAKRA BREATHING MEDITATION

This active meditation uses deep, rapid breathing and body movement to open and bring awareness, vitality and silence to each of the seven chakras* and thus into your life.
The accompanying music and bells energetically support the process and indicate the beginning of each stage. The meditation is best done on an empty stomach.

* All chakras lie deep within, rather than on the surface of the body. The following "map" is used to indicate their approximate locations:

1. *base chakra: the sex center, lower pelvis*
2. *sacral chakra: just below the navel*
3. *solar plexus chakra: above the navel, below the breastbone*
4. *heart chakra: the middle of the chest*
5. *throat chakra: the throat*
6. *third-eye chakra: between the eyebrows*
7. *crown chakra: top of the head*

This meditation is to be done with its specific OSHO Chakra Breathing Meditation music, which indicates and energetically supports the different stages. For further details, see Appendix II.

INSTRUCTIONS
The meditation lasts one hour and has two stages. Keep your eyes closed throughout.

FIRST STAGE: 45 MINUTES
Stand with your feet a little apart, your body loose and relaxed. Close your eyes and with open mouth breathe deeply and rapidly into the first chakra – your attention with each breath in the pelvic area, where the first chakra is located. Have equal emphasis on the in and the out breath. Don't force your breathing, breathe in a rhythm that feels comfortable and allows you to become aware of the feelings and sensations of each chakra.
Each time you hear a bell, move this deep, rapid breathing up to the next chakra. As you breathe up from chakra to chakra, let your breathing become more rapid and gentler, so that you are taking

about twice as many breaths in the seventh chakra than in the first. To support the breathing you can shake, stretch, rotate or move your body and hands as you feel, but let your feet stay in one spot. Allow your feet, knees, hips and other joints to become like springs so that once you set the breathing and body in motion, the movement will become continuous and effortless. Let your awareness remain primarily with the sensations of the chakras, rather than with the breathing or the body movement.
After breathing in the seventh chakra, you will hear three bells. Now let your breath and awareness turn and fall back down through each chakra, allowing your breath to become slower from chakra to chakra. Let the energy flow down by itself to include the entire spectrum of chakra energy from top to bottom, like seven colors blending into one rainbow. You have about two minutes to reach back to the first chakra and it is up to you how long you breathe into each chakra.

After you finish this sequence, stand silently for a few moments before starting the next sequence. This upward and downward breathing sequence is repeated three times.
If at first you don't feel the energy of your chakras, just breathe into the area where they are located. Remember not to push the breath – rather allow the breath and body movement to be like a bridge carrying you into the sensations and energy qualities of each chakra. Becoming sensitive to this comes through awareness and patience.

SECOND STAGE: 15 MINUTES
After the third breathing sequence, sit relaxed and in silence. Remain a witness to whatever is happening within, without judgment.

OSHO CHAKRA SOUNDS MEDITATION

This meditation can be done at any time. It uses vocal sounds to open and harmonize the chakras* or energy centers while bringing awareness to them. It can bring you into a deep, peaceful, inner silence either through making your own vocal sounds or by just listening to the music and feeling the sounds within you.

* All chakras lie deep within, rather than on the surface of the body. The following "map" is used to indicate their approximate locations:

1. *base chakra: the sex center, lower pelvis*
2. *sacral chakra: just below the navel*
3. *solar plexus chakra: above the navel, below the breastbone*
4. *heart chakra: the middle of the chest*
5. *throat chakra: the throat*
6. *third-eye chakra: between the eyebrows*
7. *crown chakra: top of the head*

This meditation is to be done with its specific OSHO Chakra Sounds Meditation music, which indicates and energetically supports the different stages. For further details, see Appendix II.

INSTRUCTIONS
The meditation lasts one hour and has two stages. Keep your eyes closed throughout.

FIRST STAGE: 45 MINUTES
Stand, sit comfortably, or lie down if you prefer. Keep your back straight and your body loose. Breathe into your belly rather than your chest. The sounds should be made with your mouth open and your jaw loose, keeping your mouth open the whole time. Close your eyes and listen to the music; if you wish, start making sounds in the first chakra. You can make a single tone or you can vary the tone. Let the music guide you; however, you can be creative with your own sounds. While listening to the sound of the music or the sounds that you make, feel the sounds pulsating in the very center of the chakra, even if it seems to be imagination at first.
Imagination can be used for "becoming attuned to something that is

already there." So keep doing the meditation even if it feels like you may be imagining the chakras. With awareness, your imagination can lead you to an experience of the inner vibrations of each center. After making sounds in the first chakra, you will hear the tones change to a higher pitch – this is the indication to listen and feel sounds in the second chakra. If you wish, you can continue making sounds also. This process is repeated all the way up to the seventh chakra. As you move from chakra to chakra, let your sounds become higher in pitch.

After listening to and making sounds in the seventh chakra, the tones will descend one at a time down through all the chakras. As you hear the tones go down, listen and make sounds in each chakra. Feel the inside of your body becoming hollow like a bamboo flute, allowing the sounds to resonate from the top of your head down to the very base of your trunk.

At the end of the sequence, you will hear a pause before the next sequence starts. This upward and downward movement of sound will be repeated three times for a total of 45 minutes.

After you have become familiar with the meditation, you can add another dimension to it through visualization – allowing visual images to appear in your imagination as you focus on each chakra. There is no need to create images, just be receptive to any which may come. The images could be colors, patterns, or scenes of nature. What comes to your awareness may be visual, or it may come as a thought – for example, you may think "gold" or you may see color in your imagination.

SECOND STAGE: 15 MINUTES
After the last sound sequence, sit or lie down with closed eyes. Remain in silence and don't focus on anything in particular. Become aware of and watch whatever is happening within – relaxed, without any judgment, remaining a witness.

Music is a very subtle meditation. The seven notes of music are concerned with the seven chakras of the body and each chakra has its own note. If you concentrate on that chakra, you will start hearing that note arising within your body. The second chakra has two notes, the third, three. One is important, the other two are just part of it but create a harmony. It goes on becoming a greater harmony, rising higher with each chakra. On the seventh chakra it is an orchestra.

Each chakra has its own form, its own music, its own taste, its own smell. The deeper you move inside yourself, the more you find the whole world because if it is not within you, you cannot see it without either. Something is needed to correspond.

OSHO PRAYER MEDITATION

In this meditation you can experience prayer as an energy phenomenon, not a devotion to God but a merging, an opening. This merging with energy is prayer. It changes you. A new élan, a new life will start penetrating you.

It is best to do the meditation at night, in a darkened room, and going to sleep immediately afterward; or it can be done in the morning, but it must then be followed by fifteen minutes rest. This rest is necessary, otherwise you will feel as if you are drunk, in a stupor.

This meditation can be done with specific OSHO Prayer Meditation music, which energetically supports it. For further details, see Appendix II.

INSTRUCTIONS
ONE STAGE WITH CYCLES OF TWO PARTS: APPROX. 20 MINUTES

Kneel, raised up on your knees, eyes closed. Raise both your arms toward the sky, the palms of your hands uppermost, head up toward the sky, just feeling existence flowing in you. As the energy or prana flows down your arms you will feel a gentle tremor. Be like a leaf in a breeze, trembling – allow it, help it. Then let your whole body vibrate with energy, and just let whatever happens, happen.

After two to three minutes or whenever you feel completely filled, lean down to the earth, resting your forehead on the ground. You simply become a vehicle to allow the divine energy to unite with that of the earth.

You feel a flowing with the earth again. Earth and heaven, above and below, yin and yang, male and female – you float, you mix, you drop yourself completely. You are not. You become one, you merge.

These two stages should be repeated six more times so that each of the chakras or energy centers can become unblocked. More times can be done, but if you do less you will feel restless and unable to sleep.

By the morning, you will feel fresher than you have ever felt before, more vital than you have ever felt before. A new élan, a new life will start penetrating you, and the whole day you will feel full of new energy; a new vibe, a new song in your heart, and a new dance in your step.

This merging with energy is prayer. It changes you. And when you change, the whole existence changes because with your attitude, the whole existence changes for you. Not that the existence is changing – existence remains the same – but now you are flowing with it, there is no antagonism. There is no fight, no struggle; you are surrendered to it.

OSHO MAHAMUDRA MEDITATION

This meditation is a meeting between you and the cosmos, between you and the whole of existence. It helps you to merge, melt and let-go on the deepest level possible.

There are two stages, with no precise timing for each. The format given below is one that works well to start with. You can do this meditation any time during the day or just before you go to sleep. If you choose to do it during the day, make sure you have some free time afterward before resuming your normal activities.

This meditation can be done with specific OSHO Mahamudra Meditation music, which indicates and energetically supports the stages. For further details, see Appendix II.

INSTRUCTIONS
The meditation lasts 45 minutes and has two stages.

FIRST STAGE: 30 MINUTES
Stand with closed eyes, allowing your body to be loose and receptive, waiting, and then cooperating when you suddenly feel an urge for your body to start moving.

When your body is relaxed and allowing, subtle energies that are outside your control begin to move it. Let your highest possibility take possession of your body and do this. Just allow it to happen. This is Latihan. And witnessing has to be joined to it, remain a witness.

SECOND STAGE: 20 MINUTES
Kneeling down, eyes closed, raise both hands toward the sky, palms upward. Feel yourself to be like a hollow bamboo or a pot. Your head is the mouth of an empty pot and tremendous energy is falling onto your head. Nothing but emptiness inside, the energy is filling you completely. Let it go as deeply as possible into your body, mind, and soul. Your body will start trembling and shaking, like a leaf in a strong wind.

When you feel filled, the energy overflowing, bend forward. Rest your forehead on the ground. Now pour the energy down into the earth. You take from the sky and give back to the earth. Just be a hollow bamboo in between, passing the energy.

Then raise your hands again, fill again, pour down again. Do it at least seven times. Each time it penetrates one chakra, one center of the body, and goes deeper. You can do more, but not less.
And this will be a complete Mahamudra.

Latihan is the first step toward Mahamudra. It is allowing the body to vibrate, allowing the body to become energy, non-substantial, nonmaterial: allowing the body to melt and dissolve its boundaries.

You have not to do anything; you have simply to be there, loose and natural, just waiting for something to happen. And if your body starts moving, you have to allow it, you just have to cooperate and allow. The cooperation should not become too direct, it should not become a pushing; it should remain just an allowing. Suddenly your body starts moving, as if you are possessed, as if a great energy from above has descended on you, as if a cloud has come and has surrounded you – and now you are possessed by that cloud, and the cloud is penetrating your body, and your body starts making movements. Your hands are raised, you make subtle movements, you start a small dance, soft gestures; your body is taken up.

And the dance is not only outside. Soon, when you get attuned to it, you will feel an inner dance also. It is not only that your body is dancing; inside the energy is dancing and they cooperate with each other. And then a pulsation happens and you feel yourself pulsating with the universe, you have found the universal rhythm.

Thirty to sixty minutes is the time: start with thirty and end with sixty. Somewhere in between you will have the right time. And you will come to know: if you feel attuned nearabout forty minutes, then that is your right time; if you feel attuned at twenty minutes, then that is your right time. Then your meditation must go beyond that: if you feel attuned at ten minutes, twenty minutes will do; if you feel attuned at fifteen minutes, thirty minutes will do. Do it double, don't take any chances, so you are really completely cleaned.

Then end it with prayerfulness. When you are completely cleaned and feeling that your body is refreshed – you have been under a shower of energy and your whole body is feeling one, undivided; and the substantialness of the body is lost, you feel it more like an energy, a movement, a process, not material – now you are ready. Then kneel down on the earth.

Raise both your hands toward the sky with closed eyes, and feel yourself like a hollow vessel, a hollow bamboo: inside, hollow, just like an earthen pot. Your head is the mouth of the pot, and tremendous energy is falling on your head as if you are standing under a waterfall.

Allow it to fall into you as deeply as possible, so it can reach the farthest corner of your body and mind and soul. And when you feel it – you are so filled, and the whole body is shaking – kneel down, put your head down on the earth, and pour the energy into the earth. When you feel the energy is overflowing, pour it down into the earth. Take from the sky; give it back to the earth, and be just a hollow bamboo in between.

This has to be done seven times. Take from the sky and pour down into the earth; kiss the earth and pour down – be completely empty. Pour down as completely as you did for filling; be completely empty. Then raise your hands again, fill again, pour down again. It has to be done seven times because each time it penetrates one chakra of the body, one center of the body; each time it goes deeper in you. And if you do it less than seven times, then you will feel restless afterward because the energy will be hanging somewhere in between.

No, it has to penetrate all seven chakras of your body so that you become completely hollow, a passage. The energy falls from the sky and goes into the earth, you are earthed; you simply pass the energy to the earth, just like electricity. For electricity we have to put an earth wire. The energy comes from the sky and goes into the earth, you become earthed: just a vessel, a hollow bamboo passing the energy. Seven times. You can do more, but not less. And this will be a complete Mahamudra.

If you do it every day, soon – somewhere within three months – one day you will feel you are not there. Just the energy is pulsating with the universe. Nobody is there, the ego is completely lost, the doer is not. The universe is there and you are there, the wave pulsating with the ocean – that is Mahamudra. That is the final orgasm, the most blissful state of consciousness that is possible.

14

HEART MEDITATIONS

Anything that has any value is never known through the head.
Love, beauty, godliness, are all known through the heart.
The heart is the gateless gate to reality.
Move from the head to the heart.
We are all hung up in the head. That is our only problem, the
one problem. And there is only one solution: get down from
the head to the heart and all problems disappear. They are
created by the head.
Suddenly everything is so clear and so transparent that one is
surprised by how one was continuously inventing problems.
Mysteries remain but problems disappear.
Mysteries abound but problems evaporate.
And mysteries are beautiful.
They are not to be solved. They have to be lived.

OSHO HEART MEDITATION

In this meditation, based on a small fragment from Atisha, the founder of Tibetan Buddhism, you allow all the suffering – of yourself and of all the beings in the world – to ride on your incoming breath and reach your heart. The heart can do miracles, it immediately transforms the energy. You drink in misery, and it is transformed into blissfulness. Then, on your outgoing breath you pour that blissfulness into the whole existence.

The meditation has no fixed format; the format given below is one that works well to start with and you can adapt it as you like later on.

This meditation can be done with specific OSHO Heart Meditation music, which indicates and energetically supports the stages. For further details, see Appendix II.

INSTRUCTIONS
The meditation lasts 50 minutes and has four stages. During the first three stages you may stand, move, sit or lie down as happens for you naturally; eyes open or closed.

FIRST STAGE: 5 MINUTES
"Moving into the heart."
Bringing your awareness to your body and breathing, feel yourself here and now.
Then bring your awareness to your heart chakra, the energy center inside the middle of your chest. If it helps you, place one or both hands on your heart center.
Absorb each in-breath into the heart, pour each out-breath out from the heart.

SECOND STAGE: 15 MINUTES
"Begin with yourself."
Start with your own misery, feel it with as much intensity as possible: the hurt, the wounds, and the suffering in your whole life. Accept it and welcome it.
Breathe in your misery... Absorb it into the heart... Let it be transformed there into joy, into bliss. Breathe out all the joy, the blissfulness; pour yourself into existence.

145

You may express in sounds, words, gestures and movements what is happening inside you or you may let it happen silently.

THIRD STAGE: 15 MINUTES
"Include all the people in the world."
Now expand this process. Take the whole misery of all beings, unconditionally – friends, enemies, family, strangers. Accept and welcome it.
Breathe in all this misery and hell... Absorb it into the heart... Let it be transformed there into joy, into bliss. Breathe out all the joy, the blissfulness; pour yourself into existence.
You may express in sounds, words, gestures and movements what is happening inside you or let it happen silently.

FOURTH STAGE: 15 MINUTES
"Come back."
Now completely withdraw your attention from the world, from others, even from yourself. Lie down, close your eyes, be silent and still.

Note: Once you experience how pain and suffering can be transformed into joy through the breath and heart, you may like to apply this method silently whenever people and events around you trigger the process.

It is one of the greatest methods. When you breathe in, think that you are breathing in all the miseries of all the people in the world. All the darkness, all the negativity, all the hell that exists anywhere, you are breathing it in. Let it be absorbed in your heart.

You may have read or heard about the so-called positive thinkers of the West. They say just the opposite – they don't know what they are saying. They say, "When you breathe out, throw out all your misery and negativity; when you breathe in, breathe in joy, positivity, happiness, cheerfulness."

Atisha's method is just the opposite: when you breathe in, breathe in all the misery and suffering of all the beings of the world – past, present and future. And when you breathe out, breathe out all the joy that you have, all the blissfulness that you have, all the benediction that you have. Breathe out, pour yourself into existence. This is the method of compassion:

drink in all the suffering and pour out all the blessings.

You will be surprised if you do it. The moment you take all the sufferings of the world inside you, they are no longer sufferings. The heart immediately transforms the energy. The heart is a transforming force: drink in misery, and it is transformed into blissfulness. Then pour it out.

Once you have learned that your heart can do this magic, this miracle, you will like to do it again and again. Try it. It is one of the most practical methods – simple, and it brings immediate results. Do it today and see.

When you take the breath in, let it become your meditation that all the suffering of all the beings in the world is riding on that incoming breath and reaching your heart. Absorb all that suffering, pain and misery in your heart and see a miracle happen.

Whenever you absorb somebody else's misery, pain and suffering, the moment you absorb it, it is transformed. The natural tendency is to avoid it; the natural tendency is to protect yourself against suffering. The natural tendency is to keep aloof, not to sympathize, not to empathize.

Everybody is burdened with great misery, everybody is in great suffering, everybody's heart is hurting. There is much pain.

Atisha says before you can do this with the whole of existence you will have to start first with yourself. This is one of the fundamental secrets of inner growth. You cannot do anything with others that you have not done in the first place with yourself. You can hurt others if you hurt yourself, you will be a pain in the necks of others if you are a pain in the neck to yourself, you can be a blessing to others only if you are a blessing to yourself.

Whatsoever you can do with others, you must have done to yourself before because that is the only thing that you can share. You can share only that which you have; you cannot share that which you don't have.

FROM THE HEAD TO THE HEART

The first point: try to be headless. Visualize yourself as headless: move headlessly. It sounds absurd, but it is one of the most,

most important exercises. Try it, and then you will know. Walk, and feel as if you have no head. In the beginning it will be "as if." It will be very weird. When the feeling comes to you that you have no head, it will be very weird and strange. But, by and by, you will settle down at the heart.

If one center is not there, energy starts moving from another.

So try this exercise I am talking about – the exercise in head-lessness – and suddenly you will feel a strange thing: as if, for the first time, you are at the heart. Walk headlessly. Sit down to meditate, close your eyes, and simply feel that there is no head: "My head has disappeared." In the beginning it will be just "as if," but, by and by, you will feel that the head has really disap-peared. And when you feel that your head has disappeared, your center will fall down to the heart – immediately. You will be look-ing at the world through the heart, not through the head.

Try headlessness. Meditate standing before your mirror in the bathroom. Look deeply into your own eyes and feel that you are looking from the heart. By and by, the heart center will begin to function. And when the heart functions, it changes your total personality, the total structure, the whole pattern, because the heart has its own way.

So the first thing: try headlessness. Secondly, be more loving because love cannot function through the head. Be more loving. That's why, when someone is in love, he loses his head. People say that he has gone mad. If you are not mad when in love, you are not really in love. The head must be lost. If the head is there unaffected, functioning ordinarily, then love is not possible because for love you need the heart to function – not the head. It is a function of the heart.

THE HEART OF PEACEFULNESS

This is a very simple method but it works miraculously – try it. And anyone can try it, there is no danger. In an easy posi-tion... The first thing is to be in a relaxed position – easy, what-soever is easy for you. So don't try some particular posture or asana. Buddha sits in a particular posture. It is easy for him. It can also become easy for you if you practice it for a time, but in the very beginning it will not be easy for you. And there is no need to practice it: start from any posture that comes easy to you right now. Don't struggle with a posture. You can sit in an easy chair and relax. The only thing is that your body must be in a relaxed state.

Just close your eyes and feel all over the body. Start from the legs, feeling whether there is any tension. If you feel somewhere there is some tension, make it tenser. If you feel that in the leg, in the right leg, there is tension, then make that tension as intense as possible. Bring it to a peak and then suddenly relax, so that you can feel how relaxation settles there. Then go all over the body, just finding if there is any tension anywhere. Wherever you feel the tension, make it more so because it is easy to relax it when it is intense. In a mid-state it is very difficult because you cannot feel it.

It is easy to move from one extreme to another, very easy, because the very extreme creates the situation to move to the other. So if you feel tension in the face, strain all the face muscles as much as possible, create tension and bring it to a peak. Bring it to a point where you feel that now no more is possible – then suddenly relax. So, see that all the parts of the body, all the limbs, are relaxed.

Be particular about the face muscles because they carry ninety percent of the tensions; the rest of the body carries only ten percent because all your tensions are in the mind and the face becomes the storage. So strain your face as much as possible, don't be shy about it. Make it intensely anguished, anxious – and then suddenly relax. Do it for five minutes so you can feel that now the whole body, every limb, is relaxed.

Find a posture that is easy for you. You can do it lying on the bed, you can do it sitting also – however you feel is easy for you.

The second thing: when you feel that the body has come to an easy posture, don't make much fuss about it. Just feel that the body is relaxed, then forget the body.

Close your eyes and just feel the area between the armpits: the heart area, your chest. First feel it, just between the armpits, and bring your total attention, total awareness. Forget the whole body, just the heart area between the armpits, the chest, and feel it filled with great peace.

The moment the body is relaxed, peace automatically happens in your heart. The heart becomes silent, relaxed, harmonious. And when you forget the whole body and bring all your attention to the chest, and consciously feel it filled with peace, much peace will happen immediately.

There are areas in the body, particular centers, where particular feelings can be created consciously. Between the armpits is the heart center, and the heart center is the source of all the peace that happens to you, whenever it happens. Whenever you are peaceful, the peace is coming from the heart. The heart radiates peace. That is why people all over the world, every race, without any distinction of caste, religion, country, cultured or uncultured, have felt that love arises from somewhere near the heart. No scientific explanation exists.

So whenever you think of love, you think of the heart. Really, whenever you are in love you are relaxed and because you are relaxed, you are filled with a certain peace. That peace arises from the heart. So peace and love have become joined, associated. Whenever you are in love you are peaceful; whenever you are not in love you are disturbed. Because of this peace, the heart has become associated with love.

So you can do two things. You can search for love, then sometimes you will feel peace. But this path is dangerous because the person you love has become more important than you. And the other is the other, and you are becoming in a way dependent. So love will give you peace sometimes but not always.

No eternal peace is possible through it, only glimpses. And between two glimpses there will be deep valleys of conflict, violence, hatred, and anger.

The other way is to find peace not through love, but directly. If you can find peace directly – and this is the method for it – your life will become filled with love. But now the quality of love will be different. It will not be possessive; it will not be centered on one. It will not be dependent and it will not make anyone dependent on you. Your love will become just a lovingness, a compassion, a deep empathy. And now no one, not even a lover, can disturb you because your peace is already rooted, and your love comes as a shadow of your inner peace. The whole thing has become reversed.

15

CENTERING MEDITATIONS

Essence is the center, that which is your nature, that which
is given by existence. Personality is the circumference, that
which is cultivated by society; it is not given by existence. It is
through nurture, not by nature.

OSHO WHIRLING MEDITATION

Whirling is an ancient Sufi technique. While your whole body is moving, you become aware of your very being, the watcher at the center, which is unmoving. You learn to be an unidentified witness at the center of the cyclone.
Whirling is best done on an empty stomach, on bare feet and wearing loose clothing.

This meditation is to be done with its specific OSHO Whirling Meditation music, which energetically supports the first stage. For further details, see Appendix II.

INSTRUCTIONS
The meditation lasts one hour and has two stages, whirling and resting.

FIRST STAGE: 45 MINUTES
The whirling is done on one spot in an anti-clockwise direction, with the right arm held high, palm upward, and the left arm low, palm downward. You whirl just like small children go on twirling. People who feel discomfort from whirling anti-clockwise can change to clockwise, changing the position of the arms as well. Let your body be soft and keep your eyes open but unfocused, so that images become blurred and flowing. Remain silent.
For the first 15 minutes, turn slowly. Then gradually build up speed until the whirling takes over and you become a whirlpool of energy – the periphery a storm of movement, the witness at the center silent and still.
When you are whirling so fast that you cannot remain upright, your body will fall by itself. Don't make the fall a decision on your part and do not try to arrange the landing in advance; if your body is soft, you will land softly and the earth will absorb your energy. Once you have fallen, stay there, this is when the second part of the meditation starts for you.

SECOND STAGE: 15 MINUTES
If you have not fallen down by the time the music stops, allow your body to fall to the ground. Immediately roll onto your stomach so that

your navel is in contact with the earth. Feel your body blending into the earth, like a small child blends into the mother's breasts. If anybody feels strong discomfort lying this way, he should lie on his back. Keep your eyes closed and remain passive and silent.

Note: Some people may feel nauseous during the Whirling Meditation, but this feeling should disappear within two or three days. Only discontinue the meditation if it persists.

OSHO NO-DIMENSIONS MEDITATION

This active centering meditation is based on Sufi techniques, and further developed and expanded by Osho. Using the breath and a series of coordinated body movements followed by whirling, your energy becomes centered in the hara, the "life energy" center below the navel. From there you can watch the mind and experience awareness and wholeness – the body moving in all directions, the center unmoving.

This meditation is to be done with its specific OSHO No-Dimensions Meditation music, which indicates and energetically supports the different stages. For further details, see Appendix II.

INSTRUCTIONS
The meditation lasts one hour and has three stages. In the first two stages the eyes are open but not focused on anything in particular. In the third stage the eyes are closed.

FIRST STAGE: 30 MINUTES
This is a six-part movement sequence, repeated continuously and accompanied by the sound "Shoo" rising from your navel to your throat. The sound helps your movements to become more free and easy as the meditation progresses. Make the movements and sounds with a loving heart and a centered awareness.
Begin by standing in one place, left hand on the heart center and right hand on the hara or navel center – until a bell rings and signals the start of the movement sequence (see demo on www.osho. com/meditations):

1. *Move both hands onto the hara, the backs of the hands touching together, pointing downward.*
    Breathing in through the nose, bring the hands up to the heart center.
    Breathing out with the sound "Shoo" move your left hand back down to the hara, and at the same time move your right arm forward (palm down) and move your right foot forward one step. Return to the original position with both hands on the hara.

2. *Repeat this same movement with the left arm and foot forward.*

Return to the original position with both hands on the hara.

3. *Repeat this movement with the right arm and foot now turning 90° sideways to the right.*
   Return to the original position with both hands on the hara.

4. *Repeat this movement with the left arm and foot now turning 90° sideways to the left.*
   Return to the original position with both hands on the hara.

5. *Repeat this movement with the right arm and foot now turning 180° clockwise to the right.*
   Return to the original position with both hands on the hara.

6. *Repeat this movement with the left arm and foot now turning 180° counter-clockwise to the left.*
   Return to the original position with both hands on the hara.

The hips and eyes always face the direction of the hand movement. Use graceful movements in a continuous flow, in rhythm with the music. This stage of the meditation starts slowly and builds up in intensity. While the music gradually becomes faster, the stillness of the center becomes more evident.

If you are doing this as a group you may get out of synchronicity with the others. When that happens, simply get back into the same rhythm as everyone else.

This stage is over when the music comes to a stop.

SECOND STAGE: 15 MINUTES
With arms folded across your chest, bow down for a few moments in loving gratitude to existence and to yourself.

Once the tempo of the music changes, begin whirling to the left or to the right, whichever feels best. If you whirl to the right, start with the right foot and right arm to the right and extend the left arm in the opposite direction. While you are whirling you can change your hands to any position that feels good to you. Whirl just like small children go on twirling.

If you have not whirled before, start out very slowly; once your mind and body get attuned to the movements the body will naturally go faster. If you get dizzy, it is okay to stop for a moment and then start again. To end the whirling, slow down with the music and again fold your arms across your heart center.

THIRD STAGE: 15 MINUTES
Lie down on the belly, eyes closed, allowing all the energy you have gathered to flow through you. If you find it uncomfortable to lie on the belly, lie on the back. There is nothing to do, just be.

Sufi Whirling is one of the most ancient techniques, one of the most forceful. It is so deep that even a single experience can make you totally different. You have to whirl with open eyes, just like small children go on twirling, as if your inner being has become a center and your whole body has become like a wheel, moving – a potter's wheel, moving. You are in the center, but the whole body is moving.

ASK YOURSELF

A Sufi mystic had remained happy his whole life. No one had ever seen him unhappy – he was always laughing. He *was* laughter, his whole being was a perfume of celebration. In his old age, when he was dying – on his deathbed, and still enjoying death, laughing hilariously – a disciple asked, "You puzzle us. Now you are dying. Why are you laughing? What is funny about it? We are feeling so sad. We wanted to ask you many times in your life why you are never sad. But now, confronting death at least, one should be sad. You are still laughing – how are you managing it?"

And the old man said, "It is simple. I had asked my master... I had gone to him as a young man: I was only seventeen and already miserable and my master was old, seventy; he was sitting under a tree, laughing for no reason at all. There was nobody else there, nothing had happened, nobody had cracked a joke or anything and he was simply laughing, holding his belly. I asked him, 'What is the matter with you? Are you mad or something?'

"He said, 'One day I was also as sad as you are. Then it dawned on me that it is my choice, it is my life.'

"Since that day, every morning when I get up, the first thing I decide is... Before I open my eyes I say to myself, 'Abdullah'" – that was his name – "'what do you want? Misery? Blissfulness? What are you going to choose today?' And it happens that I always choose blissfulness."

It is a choice. Try it. When you become aware, the first moment in the morning that sleep has left, ask yourself, "Abdullah, another day! What is your idea? Do you choose misery or blissfulness?"

Who would choose misery? And why? It is so unnatural – unless one feels blissful in misery, but then too you are choosing bliss, not misery.

FINDING THE SOURCE OF JOY

When you see a friend and suddenly feel joy arising in your heart, concentrate on this joy. Feel it and become it, and meet the friend while being aware and filled with your joy. Let the friend be just on the periphery and remain centered in your feeling of happiness.

This can be done in many other situations. The sun is rising and suddenly you feel something rising within you. Then forget the sun; let it remain on the periphery. Be centered in your own feeling of rising energy. The moment you look at it, it will spread. It will become your whole body, your whole being. And don't be just an observer of it: merge into it. There are a few moments when we feel joy, happiness, bliss, but we go on missing them because we become object-centered.

Whenever there is joy, you feel that it is coming from without. You have met a friend – of course, it appears that the joy is coming from your friend, from seeing him. That is not the actual case. The joy is always within you. The friend has just become a situation. The friend has helped it to come out, but it is there. And this is not only so with joy, but with everything: with anger, with sadness, with misery, with happiness, with everything it is so. Others are only situations in which things that are hidden in you are expressed. They are not causes; they are not causing something in you. Whatever is happening, is happening *to you*. It has always been there; it is just that meeting with this friend has become a situation in which whatever was hidden has come out in the open. It has come out from the hidden sources; it has become apparent, manifest. Whenever this happens, remain centered in the inner feeling and you will have a different attitude about everything in life.

BE UNDISTURBED

Shiva says: *"In moods of extreme desire be undisturbed."*
When desire grips you, you are disturbed. Of course, that is natural. Desire grips you, then your mind starts wavering and many ripples go on, on the surface. The desire pulls you somewhere into the future; the past pushes you somewhere into the future. You are disturbed: you are not at ease. Desire is therefore a "dis-ease."

This sutra says: *In moods of extreme desire be undisturbed.* But how to be undisturbed? Desire means disturbance, so how to be undisturbed – and in extreme moments of desire! You will have to do certain experiments; only then will you understand what is meant. You are in anger: anger grips you. You are temporarily mad, possessed; you are no longer in your senses. Suddenly, remember to be undisturbed – as if you are undressing. Inside, become naked, naked of the anger, undressed. Anger will be there, but now you have a point within you that is not disturbed.

You will know that anger is there on the periphery. Like a fever, it is there. The periphery is wavering; the periphery is disturbed, but you can look at it. If you can look at it, you will be undisturbed. Become a witness to it and you will be undisturbed. This undisturbed point is your original mind. The original mind cannot be disturbed; it is never disturbed. But you have never looked at it. When anger is there, you become identified with the anger. You forget that anger is something other than you. You become one with it, and you start acting through it, you start doing something through it.

Two things can be done. In anger you can be violent to someone, to the object of your anger. Then you have moved to the other. Anger is just in between you and the other. Here I am, there is anger, and there you are – the object of my anger.

From anger I can travel in two dimensions. I can travel to you: then you become my center of consciousness, the object of my anger. Then my mind becomes focused on you, the one who has insulted me. This is one way you can travel from anger. There is another way: you can travel to yourself. You don't move to the person whom you feel has caused the anger. You move to the person who feels to be angry; you move to the subject and not to the object.

Ordinarily, we go on moving to the object. If you move to the object, the dust part of your mind is disturbed and you will feel: "I" am disturbed. If you move within to the center of your own being, you will be able to witness the dust part: you will be able to see that the dust part of the mind is disturbed, but: "I" am not disturbed. And you can experiment on this with any desire, any disturbance.

A sexual desire comes to your mind; your whole body is taken by it. You can move to the sexual object, the object of your desire. The object may be there, it may not be there. You can move to the object in imagination also, but then you will get more and more disturbed. The further away you go from your center, the more you will be disturbed. Really, the distance and the disturbance are always in proportion. The more distant you are from your center, the more you are disturbed; the nearer you are to the center, the less you are disturbed. If you are just at the center, there is no disturbance.

In a cyclone, there is an undisturbed center – in the cyclone of anger, the cyclone of sex, the cyclone of any desire. Just in the center there is no cyclone: a cyclone cannot exist without a silent center. The anger also cannot exist without something within you which is beyond anger.

Remember: nothing can exist without its opposite. The opposite is needed. Without it there is no possibility of its existing. If there were no center within you which remains unmoved, no movement would be possible there. If there was no center within you which remains undisturbed, no disturbance could happen to you. Analyze this and observe it. If there were no center of absolute undisturbance in you, how could you feel that you are disturbed? You need a comparison. You need two points to compare.

Suppose a person is ill: he feels illness because somewhere within him, a point, a center of absolute health exists. That's why he can compare. You say that your head is aching: how is it that you know about this ache, this headache? If you were the headache, you could not know it. You must be someone else, something else – the observer, the witness who can say, "My head is aching."

This technique is not about suppression. This technique is not saying when there is anger, suppress it and remain undisturbed – no! If you suppress, you will create more disturbance. If the anger is there and the effort to suppress is there, it will double the disturbance. When anger is there, close your doors, meditate on the anger, allow the anger to be. Remain undisturbed and don't suppress it.

It is easy to suppress; it is easy to express. We do both. We express if the situation allows, if it is convenient and not dangerous. If you can harm the other and the other cannot harm you, you will express the anger. If it is dangerous, if the other can harm you more, if your boss or whoever you are angry at is stronger, you will suppress it.

Expression and suppression are easy; witnessing is difficult. Witnessing is neither: it is not suppressing, it is not expressing. It is not expressing because you are not expressing it to the object of anger. It is not being suppressed either. You are allowing it to be expressed – expressed in a vacuum. You are meditating on it.

Stand before a mirror and express your anger – and be a witness to it. You are alone, you can meditate on it. Do whatsoever you want to do, but in a vacuum. If you want to beat someone, beat toward the empty sky. If you want to be angry, be angry; if you want to scream, scream. But do it alone, and remember a point inside you that is seeing all this, this drama. Then it becomes a psychodrama, and you can laugh at it and it will be a deep catharsis for you. Afterward you will feel relieved of it – and not only relieved of it, you will have gained something through it. You will have matured; a growth comes to you. And now you know that even while you were in anger there was a center within you which was undisturbed.

16

MEDITATIONS ON LIGHT

Meditate on light and the more you meditate on light, the more
you will be surprised that something inside starts opening, as
if a bud is opening and becoming a flower.
Meditating on light is one of the most ancient meditations.
In all ages, in all countries, in all religions, it has been
emphasized for a particular reason: the moment you meditate
on light, something inside you that has remained a bud starts
opening its petals. The very meditation on light creates the
space for its opening.

OSHO GOLDEN LIGHT MEDITATION

This is a simple method of transforming your energy and leading it upward. It is best done at least twice a day, for twenty minutes each: in the morning just before getting out of bed and in the evening just before going to sleep.

This meditation can be done with specific OSHO Golden Light Meditation music, which energetically supports it. For further details, see Appendix II.

INSTRUCTIONS
ONE STAGE: 20 MINUTES
Simply lie down, as you lie down in your bed, on your back. Keep your eyes closed.

When you breathe in, just visualize great light entering through your head into your body, as if a sun has risen close to your head – golden light pouring into your head. You are just hollow and the golden light is pouring into your head, going...going...going...deep...deep, and going out through your toes.

When you breathe in, do it with this visualization.

And when you breathe out, visualize something different: darkness entering through your toes – a great, dark river entering through your toes, coming up and going out through the head. Do slow, deep breathing so you can visualize. Go very slowly.

To repeat: breathing in, let golden light come into you through your head, because it is there the Golden Flower is waiting. That golden light will help. It will cleanse your whole body and will make it absolutely full of creativity – this is male energy.

Then when you exhale, let darkness, the darkest you can conceive, like a dark night, riverlike, come upward from your toes – this is feminine energy: it will soothe you, it will make you receptive, it will calm you, it will give you rest – and let it go out of the head.

Then inhale again, and golden light enters in.

This is a simple method of transforming your energy and leading it upward.

And always remember, Taoist methods are very simple, so don't think, "How can such a simple thing be of such great importance?" Practice it, experiment with it and you will know.

The process is:

At least twice a day – the best time is early in the morning, just before you get out of bed. The moment you feel you are alert, awake, do it for twenty minutes. Do it first thing in the morning – don't get out of bed. Do it there, then and there, immediately! Because when you are coming out of sleep you are very, very delicate, receptive.

When you are coming out of sleep you are very fresh, and the impact will go very deep. When you are just coming out of your sleep you are less in the mind than ever. Hence there are some gaps through which the method will penetrate your innermost core. And early in the morning, when you are awakening and the whole earth is awakening, there is a great tide of awakening energy all over the world. Use that tide; don't miss that opportunity.

All ancient religions used to pray early in the morning when the sun rose, because the rising of the sun is the rising of all the energies in existence. In that moment you can simply ride on the rising energy wave; it will be easier. By the evening it will be difficult, the energies will be falling back. Then you will be fighting against the current, in the morning you will be going with the current.

So the best time to begin is in the early morning, immediately, just when you are half-asleep, half-awake. And the process is so simple. It needs no posture, no *yogasana*; no bath is needed, nothing.

Do it for twenty minutes early in the morning.

And then the second-best time is when you are going back to sleep at night.

Lie down on the bed, relax for a few minutes. When you start feeling that now you are wavering between sleep and waking, just in that middle, start the process again and continue for twenty minutes. If you fall asleep doing it, that is the best because the impact will remain in the subconscious and will go on working.

After a three-month period you will be surprised: the energy that was constantly gathering at the *muladhar*, at the lowest, the sex center, is no longer gathering there. It is going upward.

HEART OF LIGHT

Shiva says: *"Waking, sleeping, dreaming, know yourself as light."*

One has to start with waking. While waking – moving, eating, working – remember yourself as light, as if in your heart a flame is burning, and your body is nothing but the aura around the flame. Imagine it: in your heart a flame is burning, and your body is nothing but a light aura around the flame; your body is just a light around the flame. Allow it to go deep within your mind and your consciousness. Imbibe it.

It will take time, but if you go on thinking about it, feeling it, imagining it, within a certain period you will be able to remember it the whole day. While awake, moving on the street, you are a flame moving. No one else will be aware of it in the beginning, but if you continue it, after three months others will also become aware. Only when others become aware can you then be at ease. Don't say anything to anyone. Simply imagine a flame and your body as just the aura around it – not a physical body, but an electric body, a light body. Go on doing it.

If you persist, within three months, or somewhere nearabout then, others will become aware that something has happened to you. They will feel a subtle light around you. When you come near them, they will feel a different warmth. If you touch them, they will feel a fiery touch. They will become aware that something strange is happening to you. Don't tell anyone. When others become aware, you can feel at ease and you can enter the second step, not before.

The second step is to take it into dreaming. Now you can take it into dreaming. It has become a reality: now it is not imagination; through imagination you have uncovered a reality. It is real. Everything consists of light. You are light – unaware of the fact – because every particle of matter is light.

Scientists say it consists of electrons; it is the same thing. Light is the source of all. You are also condensed light: through imagination you are simply uncovering a reality. Imbibe it – and when you have become so filled with it, you can carry it into dreams, not before.

Then, while falling asleep, go on thinking of the flame, go on seeing it, feeling you are the light. Remembering it... Remembering... Remembering... You fall asleep and the remembrance continues. In the beginning, you will start having dreams in which you will feel you have a flame within, that you are light. By and by, in the dreams also you will move with the same feeling. And once this feeling enters the dreams, dreams will start disappearing. There will be fewer and fewer dreams and deeper and deeper sleep.

When this reality is revealed in all your dreams – that you are light, a flame, a burning flame – all dreams will disappear. Only when dreams disappear can you carry this feeling into sleep, never before. Now you are at the door. When dreams have disappeared and you remember yourself as a flame, you are at the door of sleep. Now you can enter with the feeling. And once you enter sleep with the feeling that you are a flame, you will be aware in it – the sleep will now happen only to your body, not to you.

17

MEDITATING IN DARKNESS

Just like the seed that starts its life in the darkness of the soil,
or the child that starts its life in the darkness of the womb,
all beginnings are in the dark because darkness is one of the
most essential things for anything to begin.

OSHO DARKNESS MEDITATION

This is a Tantric method. It will help you face any unconscious fear you may have of darkness and death. While doing this meditation, you create a deep friendship with darkness that enables you to enter a relaxation such as you have never known. The meditation needs to be done in a fully dark environment and you can do it for any length of time.

If you follow the one-hour format given below during the day, make sure to have some gap time afterward before driving a car or entering traffic again.

INSTRUCTIONS
The meditation lasts one hour and has two stages.

FIRST STAGE: 45 MINUTES
Sit. Remain with open eyes and stare into the blackness, into the vacuum, the darkness. Go on staring into the darkness. Feel at ease and look into it. It will start entering your eyes, and then you will start entering it.

Tears will come, your eyes may get sore, hurt – but don't get worried, just go on. The moment the darkness, the real darkness that is there, enters your eyes, it will give you a very deep, soothing feeling. You will be filled with this darkness.

SECOND STAGE: 15 MINUTES
Now lie down. Darkness is the mother of all. If everything disappears, only darkness will be there. So darkness is the mother, the womb. Feel that womb enveloping you from everywhere, and you are in it.

At the end of the hour come back, and remember, while moving, going to work, talking, eating, doing whatever, carry a patch of darkness within you. If you carry the darkness that has entered you, your whole body will become so relaxed and calm, so cool, that it will be felt.

Shiva says: *"In rain during a black night, enter that blackness as the form of forms."*

How can you enter blackness? Three things:

One: stare into blackness. Difficult. It is easy to stare at a flame, at any source of light, because it is there as an object, pointed; you can direct your attention to it. Darkness is not an object: it is everywhere, it is all around. You cannot see it as an object. Stare into the vacuum. All around it is there; just look into it. Feel at ease and look into it. It will start entering your eyes. And when the darkness enters your eyes, you are entering it.

Remain with open eyes when doing this technique in the dark night. Don't close your eyes because with closed eyes you have a different darkness that is your own, mental; it is not real. Really, it is a negative part; it is not positive darkness.

Here is light: you close your eyes and you can have darkness, but that darkness is simply the negative of the light. Just as when you look at the window and then you close your eyes, you have a negative figure of the window. All our experience is of light, so when we close our eyes we have a negative experience of light which we call darkness. It is not real, it won't do.

Open your eyes, remain with open eyes in darkness, and you will have a different darkness – the positive darkness that is there. Stare into it. Go on staring into the darkness. Your tears will start, your eyes will hurt, they will hurt. Don't get worried, just go on. And the moment the darkness, the real darkness which is there, enters your eyes, it will give you a very deep soothing feeling. When real darkness enters in you, you will be filled with it.

And this entering of darkness will empty you of all negative darkness. This is a very deep phenomenon. The darkness that you have within is a negative thing: it is against the light. It is not the absence of light; it is against the light. This is not the darkness that Shiva is speaking of as ...the form of all forms – the real darkness that's there.

We are so afraid of it that we have created many sources of light just as protection, and we live in a lighted world. Then we close our eyes and the lighted world reflects negatively inside. We have lost contact with the real darkness that is there – the darkness of the Essenes, or the darkness of Shiva. We have no contact with it. We have become so afraid of it that we have turned ourselves completely away. We are standing with our backs to it.

So this will be difficult, but if you can do it, it is miraculous, it is magical. You will have an altogether different being. When darkness enters you, you enter it. It is always reciprocal, mutual. You cannot enter any cosmic phenomenon without the cosmic phenomenon entering you. You cannot rape it, you cannot force entry. If you are available, open, vulnerable, and if you give way for any cosmic realm to enter you, only then will you enter it. It is always mutual. You cannot force it; you can only allow it.

Staying, living, with darkness for three months, one hour a day, you will lose all feeling of individuality, of separation. Then you will not be an island; you will become the ocean. You will be one with darkness. And darkness is so oceanic: nothing is so vast, nothing is so eternal. Nothing is so near you, and of nothing are you so scared and afraid. It is just at the corner, always waiting.

Stare so that it enters your eyes.

Secondly, lie down and feel as if you are near your mother. The darkness is the mother, the mother of all. Think: when there was nothing, what was there? You cannot think of anything other than darkness. If everything disappears, what will still be there? Darkness will be there.

Darkness is the mother, the womb, so lie down and feel that you are lying in the womb of your mother. And it will become real, it will become warm, and sooner or later you will start feeling that the darkness, the womb, is enveloping you from everywhere, you are in it.

And thirdly: moving, going to work, talking, eating, doing whatever, carry a patch of darkness within you. Just carry the darkness that has entered you.

Just by remembering that you are carrying darkness – you are filled with darkness, every pore of the body, every cell of the body is filled with darkness – you will feel so relaxed. Try it. You will feel so relaxed. Everything in you will be slowed down. You will not be able to run, you will walk, and that walk will be slowed down also. You will walk slowly, just as a pregnant woman walks. You will walk slowly, very carefully. You are carrying something.

Quite the opposite will happen when you are carrying a flame: your walk will become faster; rather, you would like to run. There will be more movement, you will become more active. Carrying darkness you will be relaxed. Others will start feeling that you are lazy.

Try it. It is one of the most beautiful experiences in life to carry darkness in your womb, to become dark. Walking, eating, sitting, doing whatsoever, remember, the darkness is filled in you; you are filled with it. And then see how things change. You cannot get excited, you cannot be very active, you cannot be tense. Your sleep will become so deep that dreams will disappear and the whole day you will move as if intoxicated.

18

MEDITATIONS ON SOUND

Sound exists and Tantra says sound can exist only because of silence; otherwise sound will be impossible. Silence is anti-sound. So wherever there is sound, just behind it there is silence. Just behind it – it cannot exist without it; it is the other aspect of the same coin. So, I utter a word; for example, *aum.* The moment I utter it, just side by side, just behind it is the anti-phenomenon, soundlessness.

So if you can use sounds as a technique to enter soundlessness, you will enter meditation. If you can use a word to go beyond words, you will move into meditation.

OSHO DEVAVANI MEDITATION

In this meditation a gentle, unfamiliar language moves and speaks through the meditator, who becomes an empty vessel. It deeply relaxes the mind and creates inner peace. It can be done at any time of the day. If done last thing at night, it also creates a profound sleep.

This meditation is to be done with its specific OSHO Devavani Meditation music, which energetically supports the first stage. For further details, see Appendix II.

INSTRUCTIONS
The meditation lasts one hour and has four stages. Keep your eyes closed throughout.

FIRST STAGE: 15 MINUTES
Sit quietly while the music is playing.

SECOND STAGE: 15 MINUTES
Start making nonsense sounds, for example "la la la" and continue until unfamiliar wordlike sounds arise. These sounds need to come from the unfamiliar part of the brain used as a child, before words were learned.

Allow a gentle conversational intonation; do not cry or shout, laugh or scream.

THIRD STAGE: 15 MINUTES
Stand up and continue this unfamiliar language, allowing your body to move softly in harmony with the sound. If your body is relaxed, the subtle energies will create a Latihan – a spontaneous, unstructured movement outside your control.

FOURTH STAGE: 15 MINUTES
Lie down, be silent and still.

OSHO NADABRAHMA MEDITATION
See chapter 8: OSHO Active Meditations

OSHO NADABRAHMA MEDITATION FOR COUPLES
See chapter 8: OSHO Active Meditations

OSHO TALKS
See chapter 9: OSHO Talks: Silence Shared in Words

LISTEN FROM THE HEART

When listening to music, don't listen to it from the head. Just forget your head and feel that you are headless, there is no head at all. It is good to have a picture of yourself without a head in your bedroom. Concentrate on it: you are without a head, don't allow the head to come in. While listening to music, listen to it from the heart. Let your ears be joined to the heart, not to the head. Feel it coming to your heart; let your heart vibrate with it. Try it through all the senses: feel more and more that every sense goes into the heart and dissolves into it.

AUM

Shiva says: *"Intone a sound, as aum, slowly. As sound enters soundfulness, so do you."*
    For example, take *aum*. This is one of the basic sounds. *A-U-M*: these three sounds are combined in it. *A-U-M* are three basic sounds. All sounds are made of them or derived from them; all sounds are combinations of these three sounds, so these three are basic. They are as basic as physics saying that the electron, neutron, and proton are basic. This has to be deeply understood.
    The intoning of a sound is a very subtle science. First you have to intone it loudly, outwardly; others can hear it. It is good to start loudly. Why? – because you can also hear it clearly when you intone it loudly. Whatsoever you say to others, and this has become a habit... Whenever you are talking, you are talking to others, and you hear yourself talk only when you are talking to others. So start from the natural habit.

Intone the sound *aum*, then by and by feel attunement with the sound. When you intone *aum*, be filled with it. Forget everything else. Become the *aum*, become the sound. And it is very easy to become the sound because sound can vibrate through your body, through your mind, through your whole nervous system. Feel the reverberation of *aum*. Intone it and feel it as if your whole body is being filled with it, every cell is vibrating with it.

Intoning is also "in-tuning." Tune yourself with the sound, become the sound. And then, as you feel a deep harmony between you and the sound, and you develop a deep affection for it – the sound *aum* is so beautiful and so musical – the more you intone it, the more you will feel yourself filled with a subtle sweetness. There are sounds which are bitter, there are sounds which are very hard. *Aum* is a very sweet sound, the purest. Intone it and be filled with it.

As you feel more harmonious with it, you can drop intoning loudly. Then close your lips and intone it inwardly, but inwardly also first try loudly. Intone inwardly, but loudly, so that the sound spreads all over your body, touches every part, every cell of your body. You will feel vitalized by it, you will feel rejuvenated, you will feel a new life entering you because your body is a musical instrument. It needs harmony and when the harmony is disturbed, you are disturbed.

That's why you feel good when you hear music. Why do you feel good? What is music, just harmonious sounds. Why do you feel such a well-being when there is music around you? And when there is chaos, noise, why do you feel so disturbed? You yourself are deeply musical. You are an instrument and that instrument re-echoes things.

Intone *aum* inside and you will feel that your whole body dances with it. You will feel that your whole body is under a cleansing shower; every pore is being cleansed. But as you feel it more intensely, and as it penetrates you more, go on becoming slower and slower because the slower the sound, the deeper it can go. It is just like homeopathy. The smaller the dose, the deeper it penetrates – because if you want to go deeper, you have to go more subtly, more subtly, more subtly...

Crude, coarse sounds cannot enter your heart. They can enter your ears, but they cannot enter your heart. The passage is very narrow, and the heart is so delicate that only very slow, very rhythmic, very atomic sounds are allowed to enter. And unless a sound enters your heart, the mantra is not complete. The mantra is complete only when the sound enters your heart – the deepest, most central core of your being. Then go on slower, slower, slower.

And there are also other reasons for making these sounds slower and more subtle: the more subtle a sound is, the more intense an awareness you will need to feel it inside. The coarser the sound, the less need there is of any awareness. The sound will hit you, you will become aware of it; but it is violent.

If a sound is musical, harmonious, subtle, then you will have to listen to it inside and you will have to be very alert to listen to it. If you are not alert, you will go to sleep and miss the whole point. That is the problem with a mantra, with any chanting, with any use of sound: it can create sleep. It is a subtle tranquilizer. If you continuously repeat any sound without being alert about it, you will fall asleep because the repetition becomes mechanical. "*Aum, aum, aum*" becomes mechanical, and then repetition creates boredom.

So, two things have to be done: the sound has to be slowed down and you have to become more alert. The more subtle the sound becomes, the more alert you are. To make you more alert, the sound has to be made more subtle, and a point comes when sound enters soundlessness, or soundfulness, and you enter total awareness. When the sound enters soundlessness or soundfulness, by that time your alertness must have touched the peak. When the sound reaches the valley, when it goes to the lowest, deepest center in the valley, your alertness has gone to the very peak, to Everest. And there, sound dissolves into soundfulness or soundlessness, and you dissolve into total awareness.

THE CENTER OF SOUND

Shiva says: "*Bathe in the center of sound, as in the continuous sound of a waterfall, or by putting the fingers in the ears, hear the sound of sounds.*"

This technique can be done in many ways. One way is, just sit anywhere: sounds are always present. It may be in a market or it may be at a Himalayan retreat: sounds are there. Sit silently. With sound, there is something very special: whenever there are sounds, you are the center. Whenever there are sounds, you are the center. All the sounds come to you from everywhere, from all directions.

With sight, with your eyes, this is not so. Sight is linear. I see you, then there is a line toward you. Sound is circular; it is not linear. So all sounds come in circles and you are the center. Wherever you are, you are always the center of sound. For sounds, you are always God, the center of the whole universe.

Every sound is coming to you, moving toward you, in circles.

This technique says: *bathe in the center of sound...* Wherever you are, if you are doing this technique, just close your eyes and feel the whole universe filled with sound: every sound is moving toward you and you are the center. Even this feeling that you are the center will give you a very deep peace. The whole universe becomes the circumference, and you are the center and everything is moving toward you, falling toward you: *as in the continuous sound of a waterfall...*

If you are sitting by the side of a waterfall, close your eyes and feel the sound all around you, falling on you, from every side, creating a center in you from every side. And remember why this emphasis on feeling that you are in the center. Because in the center there is no sound. The center is without sound; that is why you can hear sounds. Otherwise, you could not hear them. A sound cannot hear another sound. Because you are soundless at your center, you can hear sounds. The center is absolute silence: that is why you can hear sounds entering you, coming to you, penetrating you, encircling you.

If you can find where the center is, where every sound is coming to inside you, suddenly sounds will disappear and you will enter soundlessness. If you can feel a center where every sound is being heard, there is a sudden transference of consciousness. One moment you will be hearing the whole world filled with sounds, and another moment your awareness will suddenly turn in and you will hear the soundlessness, the center of life.

Once you have heard that, no sound can disturb you. It comes to you, but it never reaches you. It comes to you, it is always coming to you, but it never reaches you. There is a point where no sound enters. That point is you.

19

THE ART OF LOOKING

Looking at the sky full of stars, suddenly you feel so contented
– what more can there be? It cannot be improved upon.
The starry night is so breathtaking.
The sunset for a moment stops your heartbeat.
A bird on the wing – and suddenly your mind is not there.
These are natural glimpses of meditation.

OSHO TALKS
See chapter 9: OSHO Talks: Silence Shared in Words

LOOK WITHOUT WORDS

Look at a flower and don't say anything. It will be difficult, the mind will feel uneasy because it has become habitual. It constantly goes on chattering. Look at a flower and make it a meditation. Look at a tree and don't name it, don't say anything. There is no need; the tree is there, why say anything?

I have heard it happened: Lao Tzu, one of the greatest Chinese mystics, used to go for a walk every morning. A neighbor used to follow him, but the neighbor knew that Lao Tzu was a man of silence, so for years he followed him on the morning walk but he never said anything. One day, there was a visitor at the neighbor's house, a guest, and he also wanted to come. The neighbor said, "Don't say anything because Lao Tzu wants to live directly. Don't say anything!"

They went out, and the morning was so beautiful, so silent, the birds were singing, and just out of habit the guest said, "How beautiful!" Just this much, nothing much; for a one-hour walk, this is not very much: "How beautiful!" But Lao Tzu looked at him as if he had committed a sin.

Back home, going in his door, Lao Tzu said to the neighbor, "Never come again! And never bring anybody else: this man seems to be so talkative."

And he had only said, "How beautiful!"

Too talkative.

Lao Tzu said, "The morning was beautiful, it was so silent. This man disturbed the whole thing."

"How beautiful!" It fell like a stone in a silent pool. "How beautiful!" fell like a stone in a silent pool and the whole thing rippled...

Meditate near a tree, meditate with the stars, with a river, with the ocean, meditate in the market, people passing. Don't say anything, don't judge, don't use words: just look. If you can clear your perception, if you can attain a clarity of looking, everything is achieved. And once this clarity is achieved, you will be able to see yourself.

LOOK WITH EMPTY EYES

Meditate on the moon more and more. Whenever the moon is in the sky, just sit looking at it, but with very empty eyes. Looking and yet not concentrating. Just looking, but with no strain. Do you follow?

The look can be of two types. One look is what we call attention: you focus – and there is a strain in the mind, as if you are going to hit the target with an arrow. Then you concentrate. But that is not right. Just look relaxedly, as if you are looking by the way and the moon is there.

Look at the moon with empty eyes.

SEEING FOR THE FIRST TIME

We always look at things with old eyes. You come to your home; you look at it without looking at it. You know it – there is no need to look at it. You have entered it again and again for years together. You go to the door, you enter; you may unlock the door. But there is no need to look.

This whole process goes on robotlike, mechanical, unconscious. If something goes wrong, only if your key is not fitting the lock, then you look at the lock. If the key fits, you never look at the lock. Because of mechanical habits, repeatedly doing the same thing again and again, you lose the capacity to look; you lose the freshness to look. Really, you lose the function of your eyes – remember this. You become basically blind because eyes are not needed.

Remember the last time you looked at your wife. The last time you looked at your wife or at your husband may have been years ago. For how many years have you not looked? You just pass by, a casual glimpse, but not a look. Go again and look at your wife or at your husband as if you were looking for the first time. Why? – because if you are looking for the first time, your eyes will be filled with freshness. They will become alive.

You are walking through a street and a beautiful woman passes by. Your eyes become alive – lighted. A sudden flame comes to them. This woman may be a wife to someone. He will not look at her; he may become as alive as you have become, seeing *your* wife. Why? The first time, eyes are needed, the second time not so much, and the third time they are not needed. After a few repetitions you become blind. We live blindly.

Be aware. When you meet your children, are you looking at them? You are not looking at them. This habit kills the eyes; the eyes become bored – the old again and again. And nothing is old really, it is just that your habit makes you feel so. Your wife is not the same as she was yesterday, she cannot be; otherwise she is a miracle. Nothing can be the same the next moment. Life is a flux, everything is flowing, nothing is the same.

The same sunrise will not happen again. In a very physical sense also, the sun is not the same. Every day it is new; basic changes have occurred. And the sky will not be the same again; this morning is not going to come again. Every morning has its own individuality, and the sky and the colors will not gather in the same pattern again. But you go on moving as if everything is just the same. They say nothing is new under the sky. Really, nothing is old under the sky. Only the eyes become old, accustomed; then nothing is new.

Look at everything you pass as if for the first time. Make it a continuous attitude. Touch everything as if for the first time. What will happen? If you can do this, you will be freed from your past. The burden, the dust, the dirtiness, the accumulated experiences – you will be freed from them.

Every moment, move away from the past. Don't allow it to enter within you; don't allow it to be carried – leave it. Look at everything as if for the first time. This is a great technique to help you to be freed from the past. Then you are constantly in the present, and by and by you will have an affinity with the present. Then everything is new. Then you will be able to understand Heraclitus' saying that you cannot step twice in the same river.

FEEL THE LIGHT RETURNING

Lu-tsu says: *"When the light is made to move in a circle, all the energies of heaven and earth, of the light and the dark, are crystallized."*

Just standing before a mirror someday, try a small experiment. You are looking in the mirror, your own face in the mirror, your own eyes in the mirror. This is extroversion: you are looking into the mirrored face – your own face, of course, but it is an object outside you. Then, for a moment, turn the whole process. Start feeling that you are being looked at by the reflection in the mirror – not that you are looking at the reflection, but the reflection is looking at you – and you will be in a very strange space. Just try it for a few minutes and you will be very alive, and something of immense power will start entering you. You may even become frightened because you have never known it, you have never seen the complete circle of energy.

In the beginning it may be frightening because you have never done it and you have never known it; it will look crazy. You may feel shaken, a trembling may arise in you, or you may feel disoriented because your whole orientation up to now has been extroversion. Introversion has to be learned slowly, slowly. But the circle is complete. And if you do it for a few days you will be surprised how much more alive you feel the whole day – just a few minutes standing before the mirror and letting the energy come back to you so the circle is complete. Whenever the circle is complete there is a great silence. The incomplete circle creates restlessness. When the circle is complete it creates rest, it makes you centered. And to be centered is to be powerful – the power is yours.

This is just an experiment; then you can try it in many ways.

Looking at a roseflower, first look at the roseflower for a few moments, a few minutes, and then start the reverse process: the roseflower is looking at you. And you will be surprised how much energy the roseflower can give to you. The same can be done with trees and stars and with people. And the best way is to do it with the woman or man you love. Just look into each other's eyes. First begin looking at the other and then start feeling the other is returning the energy to you; the gift is coming back. You will feel replenished, you will feel showered, bathed, basked in a new kind of energy. You will come out of it rejuvenated, vitalized.

20

MEDITATIONS ON TOUCH

Be sensitive to your being.
When you touch someone's hand,
don't only touch his hand, feel your touch also,
feel yourself also – that you are here in this touch,
totally present.

TOUCHING LIKE A FEATHER

Shiva says: *"Touching eyeballs as a feather, lightness between them opens into heart and there permeates the cosmos."*

Use both your palms, put them on your closed eyes and allow the palms to touch the eyeballs – but just like a feather, with no pressure. If you press, you miss the point, you miss the whole technique. Don't press; just touch like a feather. You will have to adjust because in the beginning you will be pressing. Find less and less pressure, just touching with no pressure at all – your palms just touch the eyeballs. Just a touch, just a meeting; no pressure because if there is pressure, the technique will not function. Like a feather.

Why? – because a needle can do something which a sword cannot do. If you press, the quality has changed – you are aggressive. And the energy that is flowing through the eyes is very subtle: a small pressure and it starts fighting and a resistance is created. If you press, then the energy that is flowing through the eyes will start resistance, fight; a struggle will ensue. So don't press. Even a slight pressure is enough for the eye energy to judge.

It is very subtle, it is very delicate. Don't press – like a feather, just your palm is touching, as if not touching. Touching as if not touching, no pressure; just a touch, a slight feeling that the palm is touching the eyeball, that's all.

What will happen? When you simply touch without any pressure, the energy starts moving within. If you press, it starts fighting with the hand, with the palm, and moves out. Just a touch and the energy starts moving within. The door is closed; simply the door is closed and the energy falls back. The moment energy falls back, you will feel a lightness coming all over your face, your head. This energy moving back makes you light.

And just between these two eyes is the third eye, the wisdom eye, the *prajna-chakshu*. Just between the two eyes is the third eye. The energy falling back from the eyes hits the third eye. That's why one feels light, levitating, as if there is no gravitation. And from the third eye the energy falls on the heart. It is a physical process: just drip, drip, it drops, and you will feel a very light feeling entering your heart. The heartbeats will slow down, the breathing will slow down. Your whole body will feel relaxed.

Even if you are not entering deep meditation, this will help you physically. Any time during the day, relax on a chair – or if you don't have a chair, just sitting in a train – close your eyes, feel a relaxation in the whole of your body, and then put both your palms on your eyes. But don't press – that's the very significant thing. Just touch like a feather.

When you touch and don't press, your thoughts will stop immediately. In a relaxed mind, thoughts cannot move; they get frozen. They need frenzy and fever, they need tension to move. They live through tension. When the eyes are silent, relaxed, and the energy is moving backward, thoughts will stop. You will feel a certain quality of euphoria and it will deepen daily.

So do it many times in the day. Even for a single moment, touching will be good. Whenever your eyes feel exhausted, dry of energy, exploited – reading, seeing a film, or watching TV – whenever you feel it, just close the eyes and touch. Immediately there will be the effect. But if you want to make it a meditation, then do it for at least forty minutes.

TOUCH FROM INSIDE YOUR BODY

You have seen your body only from outside. You have seen your body in a mirror or you have seen your hands from the outside. You don't know what the inside of your body is. You have never entered your own self; you have never been at the center of your body and being, to look around at what is there from the inside.

This technique is very helpful to have a look from the inside, and that transforms your total consciousness, your total existence – because if you can have a look from the inside, you immediately become different from the body.

Close your eyes, see your inner being in detail and move from limb to limb inside. Just go to your toe. Forget the whole body: move to the toe. Stay there and have a look. Then move through the legs, come on upward, go to every limb. Then many things happen. *Many* things happen!

Then your body becomes such a sensitive vehicle, you cannot even imagine it. Then, if you touch someone, you can move into your hand totally and that touch will become transforming.

FEEL THE TOUCH

So when such techniques have to be practiced, the first difficulty will be that you don't know what feeling is. Try to develop it. When you touch something, close your eyes; don't think, feel. For example, if I take your hand in my hand and I say to you, "Close your eyes and feel what is happening," immediately you will say, "Your hand is in my hand." But this is not a feeling, this is a thinking.

Then I again say to you, "Feel. Don't think." Then you say, "You are expressing your love." That is again thinking. If I insist again, "Just feel, don't use your head. What are you feeling right now?" only then will you be able to feel and say, "The warmth." Because love is a conclusion. "Your hand is in my hand" – this is a head-oriented thought.

The actual feeling is that a certain warmth is flowing from my hand to your hand, or from your hand to my hand. Our life energies are meeting and the point of meeting has become hot, it has become warm. This is the feeling, the sensation, the real. But we go on continuously with the head. It has become a habit; we are trained for it. So you will have to re-open your heart.

Try to live with feelings. Sometimes in the day when you are not doing any particular business – because at work, in the beginning it will be difficult to live with feelings. There, the head has proved very efficient and you cannot depend on feeling. While you are at home playing with your children, the head is not needed, it is not a business – but there too you are with the head. Playing with your children or just sitting with your wife, or not doing anything, relaxing in a chair, feel. Feel the texture of the chair.

Your hand is touching the chair: how are you feeling it? The air is blowing, the breeze is coming in. It touches you. How do you feel? Smells are coming from the kitchen. How do you feel? Just feel. Don't think about them. Don't start brooding that the smell shows that something is being prepared in the kitchen – then you will start dreaming about it. No, just feel whatsoever is the fact. Remain with the fact; don't move into thinking.

TOUCH FROM THE HEART

You touch someone: if you are a heart-oriented person, the touch immediately goes to your heart and you can feel their quality. If you take the hand of a person who is head-oriented, the hand will be cold – not just cold, the very quality will be cold. A deadness, a certain deadness will be there in the hand. If the person is heart-oriented, there is a certain warmth, his hand will really melt with you. You will feel something flowing from his hand to you, and there will be a meeting, a communication of warmth.

This warmth comes from the heart. It can never come from the head because the head is always cool, cold, calculating. The heart is warm, non-calculative. The head always thinks about how to take more; the heart always feels how to give more. That warmth is just a giving – a giving of energy, a giving of inner vibrations, a giving of life. That is why you feel a different quality in it. If someone really embraces you, you will feel a deep melting with him.

Touch! Close your eyes; touch anything. Touch your beloved or your lover, touch your child or your mother or your friend, or touch a tree or a flower, or just touch the earth. Close your eyes and feel a communication from your heart to the earth or to your beloved. Feel that your hand is just your heart stretched out to touch the earth. Let the feeling of touch be related to the heart.

Let your love be your state of being. Not that you fall in love, but just that you are loving. It is simply your nature. Love, to you, is just the fragrance of your being. Even if you are alone, you are surrounded by loving energy. Even if you touch a dead thing, like the chair, your hand is showering love – it does not matter to whom.

21

FINDING SPACE INSIDE

When your inner space is totally free from all junk – words,
thoughts, memories, desires, dreams, imaginations – when all
are gone and you are simply there, silently there, experiencing
this tremendous nothingness,
that is the moment when bliss is felt for the first time.

ENTER THE CLEAR SKY

Meditate on the sky; a summer sky with no clouds, endlessly empty and clear, nothing moving in it, in its total virginity. Contemplate on it, meditate on it, and enter this clarity. Become this clarity, this spacelike clarity.

If you meditate on open, unclouded sky, suddenly you will feel that the mind is disappearing, the mind is dropping away. There will be gaps. Suddenly you will become aware, as if the clear sky has entered you also. There will be intervals. For the time being, thoughts will cease – as if the traffic has ceased and there is no one moving.

In the beginning it will be only for moments, but even those moments are transforming. By and by, the mind will slow down, bigger gaps will appear. For minutes together there will be no thought, no cloud. And when there *is* no thought, no cloud, the outer sky and the inner become one because only the thought is the barrier, only the thought creates the wall. The outer is outer and the inner is inner only because of thought. When the thought is not there, the outer and the inner lose their boundaries, they become one. Really, boundaries never existed. They appeared only because of the thought, the barrier.

To meditate on the sky is beautiful. Just lie down so you forget the earth; just lie down on your back on any lonely beach, on any ground, and just look at the sky. A clear sky will be helpful – unclouded, endless. Just looking, staring at the sky, feel the clarity of it – the uncloudedness, the boundless expanse and then enter that clarity, become one with it. Feel as if you have become the sky, the space.

First you enter into the sky and then the sky enters you. And there is a meeting: the inner sky meeting the outer sky. In that meeting is realization. In that meeting there is no mind because the meeting can happen only when the mind is not there. In that meeting you are for the first time not your mind. There is no confusion. Confusion cannot exist without the mind. There is no misery because misery also cannot exist without the mind.

This technique of looking into the clarity of the sky and becoming one with it is one of the most practiced. Many traditions have used it. And it will be very useful particularly for the modern mind because on earth, nothing is left. Nothing is left on earth to meditate on – only the sky. If you look all around, everything is man-made, everything is limited, with a boundary, a limitation. Only the sky is fortunately still open to meditate on.

Try this technique, it will be helpful, but remember three things. One: don't blink – stare. Even if your eyes start to feel pain and tears come down, don't be worried. Even the tears will be a part of unloading; they will be helpful. Those tears will make your eyes more innocent and fresh, bathed. Just go on staring.

The second point: don't think about the sky, remember. You can start thinking about the sky. You can remember many poems, beautiful poems about the sky – then you will miss the point. You are not to think about it – you are to enter it, you are to be one with it – because if you start thinking about it, again a barrier is created. You are missing the sky again, you are enclosed in your own mind again. Don't think about the sky. Be the sky. Just stare and move into the sky, and allow the sky to move into you. If you move into the sky, the sky will move into you immediately.

How can you do it? How will you do it? Just go on staring far away, far away... Just go on staring. Go on staring as if you are trying to find the boundary. Move deep. Move as much as you can. That very movement will break the barrier. And this method should be practiced for at least forty minutes; less than that will not do, will not be of much help.

When you really feel that you have become one, then you can close your eyes. When the sky has entered you, you can close your eyes. You will be able to see it within also. So only after forty minutes, when you feel that the oneness has happened and there is a communion and you have become part of it and the mind is no more, close your eyes and remain in the sky within.

The clarity will help the third point: enter such clarity. The clarity will help: the uncontaminated, unclouded sky. Just be aware of the clarity that is all around you. Don't think about it, just be aware of the clarity, the purity, the innocence. These words are not to be repeated. You have to feel them rather than think. And once you stare into the sky, the feeling will come because it is not on your part to imagine these things – they are there. If you stare they will start happening to you.

But what will you do if it is not summer? If the sky is clouded, not clear, then close your eyes and just enter the inner sky. Just close your eyes and if you see some thoughts, just see them as if they are floating clouds in the sky. Be aware of the background, the sky, and be indifferent to thoughts.

INCLUDE EVERYTHING

Sitting in meditation, be inclusive of all – your body, your mind, your breath, your thinking, your knowing, everything. Be inclusive of all. Don't divide, don't create any fragmentation. Ordinarily we are fragmenting; we go on fragmenting. We say, "The body is not me." There are techniques which can use that also, but this technique is totally different, rather it is the opposite.

Don't divide. Don't say, "I am not the body." Don't say, "I am not the breath." Don't say, "I am not the mind." Just say, "I am all" – and be all. Don't create any fragmentation within you. This is a feeling. With closed eyes include everything that exists in you. Don't get yourself centered anywhere – be uncentered. The breath comes and goes, thought comes and moves. The form of your body will go on changing. You have not observed this.

If you sit with closed eyes, you will feel that sometimes your body is big, sometimes your body is small; sometimes it is very heavy, sometimes just light, as if you can fly. You can feel this increasing and decreasing of the form. Just close your eyes and sit and you will feel that sometimes the body is very big – filling the whole room; sometimes it is so small – just atomic. Why does this form change? As your attention changes, the form of the body changes. If you are inclusive, it will become big; if you exclude – "This is not I, this is not I" – then it will become very minute, very small, atomic.

Include everything in your being and don't discard anything. Don't say, "This is not I." Say, "I am," and include everything in it. If you can do this just sitting, wonderful, absolutely new happenings will happen to you. You will feel there is no center; in you there is no center. And with the center gone, there is no self, there is no ego; only consciousness remains – consciousness like a sky covering everything. And when it grows, not only your own breath will be included, not only your own form will be included; ultimately the whole universe becomes inclusive to you.

The basic point is to remember inclusiveness. Don't exclude. This is the key for this technique – inclusiveness, include. Include and grow. Include and expand. Try it with your body and then try it with the outside world also.

Sitting under a tree, look at the tree, then close your eyes and feel that the tree is within you. Look at the sky, then close your eyes and feel that the sky is within you. Look at the rising sun, then close your eyes and feel that the sun is rising within you. Feel more inclusive.

A tremendous experience will happen to you. When you feel that the tree is within you, immediately you will feel younger, fresher. And it is not imagination because the tree and you both belong to the earth. You are both rooted in the same earth and ultimately rooted in the same existence. So when you feel that the tree is within you, the tree *is* within you – this is not imagination – and immediately you will feel the effect. The tree's aliveness, the greenery, the freshness, the breeze passing through it, will be felt within you in your heart. Include more and more of existence and don't exclude.

And remember this: make it a lifestyle to include – not only in meditation, but a lifestyle, a way of living. Try to include more and more. The more you include, the more you expand, the more your boundaries recede to the very corners of existence. One day only you are; the whole existence is included. This is the ultimate of all religious experience.

FEEL THE ABSENCE OF THINGS

Patanjali says: "*On attaining the utmost purity of the nirvichara stage of samadhi, there is a dawning of the spiritual light.*"

Your innermost being is of the nature of light. Consciousness is light; consciousness is the only light. You are existing very unconsciously: doing things, not knowing why; desiring things, not knowing why; asking things, not knowing why – drifting in an unconscious sleep. You are all sleepwalkers. Somnambulism is the only spiritual disease: walking and living in sleep. Become more conscious.

Start being conscious with objects. Look at things with more alertness. You pass by a tree, look at the tree with more alertness. Stop for a while, look at the tree; rub your eyes, look at the tree with more alertness. Collect your awareness, look at the tree and watch the difference. Suddenly, when you are alert, the tree is different – it is more green, it is more alive, it is more beautiful. The tree is the same, only you have changed. Look at a flower as if your whole existence depends on this look. Bring all your awareness to the flower and suddenly the flower is transfigured – it is more radiant, it is more luminous. It has something of the glory of the eternal, as if the eternal has come into the temporal in the shape of a flower.

Look at the face of your husband, your wife, your friend, your beloved, with alertness; meditate on it and suddenly you see not only the body, but that which is beyond the body, which is coming out of the body. There is an aura around the body, of the spiritual. The face of the beloved is no longer the face of your beloved; the face of the beloved has become the face of the divine. Look at your child. Watch him playing with full alertness, awareness, and suddenly the object is transfigured.

Start with objects and move toward more subtle objects. For example, a bird sings in the tree: be alert, as if in that moment only you and the song of the bird exist – the whole bird doesn't exist, doesn't matter. Focus your being toward the song of the bird and you will see the difference. The traffic noise no longer exists, or exists at the very periphery of existence, far away, distant, and the small bird and its song fills your being completely – only you and the bird exist. And then when the song has stopped, listen to the absence of the song. Then the object becomes subtle because...

Remember always: when a song stops, it leaves a certain quality to the atmosphere – of the absence. It is no longer the same. The atmosphere has changed completely because the song existed, and then the song disappears. Now the absence of the song... Watch it – the whole existence is filled with the absence of the song, and it is more beautiful than any song because it is the song of the silence. A song uses sound and when the sound disappears, the absence uses the silence. After a bird has sung, the silence is deeper. If you can watch it, if you can be alert, you are now meditating on a very subtle object, a *very* subtle object.

A person moves, a beautiful person moves – watch that person. When he has left, now watch the absence; he has left something. His energy has changed the room; it is no longer the same room.

If you have a good nose... Very few people have, humanity has almost lost the nose completely. Animals are better, their sense of smell is far more sensitive, capable, than man's. Something has happened to man's nose, something has gone wrong; very few people have a capable nose, but if you have, then be near a flower, let the smell fill you. Then, by and by, move away from the flower – very slowly, but continue being attentive to the smell, to the fragrance. As you move away, the fragrance will become more and more subtle and you will need more awareness to feel it. Become the nose. Forget about the whole body, bring all your energy to the nose, as if only the nose exists. By and by, if you lose track of the smell, go a few steps forward, again catch hold of the smell; then back, move backward. By and by, you will be able to smell a flower from a very, very great distance – nobody will be able to smell that flower from there. Then go on moving. In a very simple way you are making the object subtle.

A moment will come when you will not be able to smell the smell: now smell the absence. Now smell the absence where the fragrance was just a moment before and is no longer. That is the other part of its being, the absent part, the dark part. If you can smell the absence of the smell, if you can feel it, feel that it makes a difference, it *makes* a difference; then the object has become very subtle.

You can do it with incense. Burn incense, meditate on it, feel it, smell it, be filled with it, and then move backward away from it – and go on, go on meditating on it; let it become more and more subtle. A moment comes when you can feel the absence of a certain thing. Then you have come to a very deep awareness.

"*On attaining the utmost purity of the nirvichara stage of samadhi, there is a dawning of the spiritual light.*" But when the object completely disappears – the presence of the object disappears and the absence of the object disappears; thought disappears and no-thought disappears; mind disappears and the idea of no-mind disappears – only then have you attained the utmost.

Now this is the moment when grace suddenly descends on you. This is the moment when flowers shower. This is the moment when you are connected with the source of life and being.

HOLLOW BAMBOO

Tilopa says: *"Like a hollow bamboo rest at ease with your body."*

This is one of Tilopa's special methods. Every master has his own special method through which he has attained, and through which he would like to help others. This is Tilopa's specialty: *Like a hollow bamboo rest at ease with your body.*

A bamboo: inside, completely hollow. When you rest, just feel that you are like a bamboo: inside completely hollow and empty. And in fact this is the case: your body is just like a bamboo, and inside it is hollow. Your skin, your bones, your blood, are all part of the bamboo, and inside there is space, hollowness.

When you are sitting with a completely silent mouth, inactive, tongue touching the roof and silent, not quivering with thoughts, mind watching passively, not waiting for anything in particular, feel like a hollow bamboo – and suddenly infinite energy starts pouring within you, you are filled with the unknown, with the mysterious, with the divine. A hollow bamboo becomes a flute and the divine starts playing it. Once you are empty, there is no barrier for the divine to enter you.

Try this; it is one of the most beautiful meditations, the meditation of becoming a hollow bamboo. You need not do anything else. Simply become it – and all else happens. Suddenly you feel something is descending into your hollowness. You are like a womb and a new life is entering you, a seed is falling. And a moment comes when the bamboo completely disappears.

22

EMPTYING THE MIND

There is no such thing as peace of mind.
There is only one peace and that is when there is no mind.
When there is only a watcher and nothing to watch,
suddenly everything becomes calm and quiet.

—

When the mind disappears, thoughts disappear.
It is not that you become mindless; on the contrary, you
become mindful. Buddha uses the words "right mindfulness"
millions of times. When the mind disappears and thoughts
disappear, you become mindful.
You do things – you move, you work, you eat, you sleep,
but you are always mindful.
The mind is not there, but mindfulness is there.
What is mindfulness?
It is awareness. It is perfect awareness.

OSHO GIBBERISH MEDITATION

Gibberish is one of the most scientific ways to clean your mind. This is a cathartic technique which encourages expressive sounds and body movements, followed by a deep merging or a silent relaxation.

INSTRUCTIONS
The meditation lasts 30 minutes and has two stages. For the second stage two options are given and you can choose whichever fits best in the moment.

FIRST STAGE: 15 MINUTES
Either alone or in a group, close your eyes and start to say whatever needs to be expressed within you – everything that you ever wanted to say and have not been able to say because of civilization, education, culture, society. Just do it totally, enthusiastically. Anything that is moving in your mind, throw it out. Just avoid the language that you know. If you don't know Chinese, say it in Chinese! Use Japanese if you don't know Japanese. Don't use German if you know German.
Bring out all your craziness in rubbish, gibberish, sounds, gestures.
Simply allow whatever comes to your mind without bothering about its rationality, reasonability, meaning, significance. For the first time have a freedom – the same as all the birds have.
The mind always thinks in terms of words. Gibberish helps to break this pattern of continual verbalization. Don't be bothered whether it is Arabic or Hebrew or Chinese, you are allowed to speak any language that you don't know. Just avoid the language that you do know, because the language that you do know will not bring your nonsense out. Without suppressing your thoughts, you can throw them out – in gibberish. And likewise, let your body be expressive. Be sincere, make it a reality. Just go crazy.

SECOND STAGE: 15 MINUTES – OPTION 1
Lie down on your stomach and feel as if you are merging with Mother Earth. With each exhalation, feel yourself merging with the ground beneath you.

SECOND STAGE: 15 MINUTES – OPTION 2
Silently relax – sitting, with closed eyes, watching the inner sky.

Note: For more understanding of gibberish, see also the "OSHO No-Mind" section in chapter 11: OSHO Meditative Therapies, and the "A: Gibberish" section in chapter 10: OSHO Evening Meeting Meditation.

I am dealing with the contemporary man, who is the most restless being that has ever evolved on the earth. But people do become silent; you just have to allow them to throw out their madness, insanity, then they themselves become silent.

Gibberish should be taught to every person. The world will become saner if you can simply sit in your room and talk loudly to nobody in particular for one hour. In the beginning it will look crazy. It is! But it will relieve you of much heat, steam, and after one hour you will feel tremendously quiet.

And it is inhuman to force your gibberish on other people, because you *can* force it on them. Then they are in trouble: whatever you have said to them goes on rumbling inside their head; they have to search for somebody else, and on and on. This way the problem that could have been solved becomes a world problem! You may be gone, but the gibberish that you have put in other people's heads will go on and on for centuries. There is no way to end it; then a full stop cannot be put to it.

If you want to throw out your junk, please make it a point not to throw it on any other human being. People have their own already, and it is too much; don't add to it.

But you can go to a river and talk to the river. The river won't listen, so there is no problem: the river won't go mad. You can go to a tree and talk to the tree, and you can talk to the stars, and you can talk to the walls; that's perfectly good. And if you feel it is too crazy, then write it down: make a diary and write all that you want.

You have to get rid of your steam, but it should not enter anybody else's being; otherwise you are violent. And if people learn this simple thing, the world will become saner.

OSHO NO-MIND
See chapter 11: OSHO Meditative Therapies

THROWING THINGS OUT

Patanjali says: "*The mind also becomes tranquil by alternately expelling and retaining the breath.*"
      Whenever you feel that the mind is not tranquil – tense, worried, chattering, anxious, constantly dreaming – do one thing: first exhale deeply. Always start by exhaling. Exhale deeply; as much as you can, throw the air out. Throwing out the air, the mood will be thrown out too because breathing is everything.
      Expel the breath as far as possible. Pull the belly in and retain for a few seconds; don't inhale. Let the air be out, and don't inhale for a few seconds. Then allow the body to inhale. Inhale deeply – as much as you can. Again stop for a few seconds. The gap should be the same as when breathing out – if you held it for three seconds, hold the breath in for three seconds. Throw it out and hold for three seconds; take it in and hold for three seconds.
      But the breath has to be thrown out completely. Exhale totally and inhale totally, and make a rhythm. Hold, then breathe in; hold, then breathe out. Hold, in; hold, out. Immediately you will feel a change coming into your whole being. The mood has gone; a new climate has entered you.

HOW TO STOP THINKING

Thinking cannot be stopped. Not that it does not stop, but it cannot be stopped. It stops of its own accord. This distinction has to be understood, otherwise you can go mad chasing your mind.
      No-mind does not arise by stopping thinking. When the thinking is no more, no-mind is. The very effort to stop it will create more anxiety, it will create conflict, it will make you split. You will be in a constant turmoil within. This is not going to help.
      And even if you succeed in stopping it forcibly for a few moments, it is not an achievement at all – because those few moments will be almost dead, they will not be alive. You may feel a sort of stillness, but not silence because a forced stillness is not

silence. Underneath it, deep in the unconscious, the repressed mind goes on working.

So, there is no way to stop the mind. But the mind stops – that is certain. It stops of its own accord. So what to do? The question is relevant. Watch – don't try to stop. There is no need to do any action against the mind. In the first place, who will do it? It will be mind fighting mind itself. You will divide your mind into two; one that is the top-dog, trying to boss, trying to kill the other part of itself, which is absurd. It is a foolish game. It can drive you crazy. Don't try to stop the mind or the thinking – just watch it, allow it. Allow it total freedom. Let it run as fast as it wants. Don't try in any way to control it. Just be a witness. It is beautiful.

The mind is one of the most beautiful mechanisms. Science has not yet been able to create anything parallel to it. The mind still remains the masterpiece – so complicated, so tremendously powerful, with so much potential. Watch it, enjoy it!

And don't watch like an enemy because if you look at the mind like an enemy, you cannot watch. You are already prejudiced; you are already against. You have already decided that something is wrong with the mind – you have already concluded. And whenever you look at somebody as an enemy you never look deep, you never look into their eyes. You avoid.

Watching the mind means: look at it with deep love, with deep respect, reverence – it is existence's gift to you. Nothing is wrong in the mind itself. Nothing is wrong in thinking itself. It is a beautiful process, as other processes are. Clouds moving in the sky are beautiful – why not thoughts moving in the inner sky? Flowers coming to the trees are beautiful – why not thoughts flowering in your being? The river running to the ocean is beautiful – why not this stream of thoughts running somewhere to an unknown destiny? Is it not beautiful?

Look with deep reverence. Don't be a fighter, be a lover. Watch the subtle nuances of the mind; the sudden turns, the beautiful turns, the sudden jumps and leaps; the games that the mind goes on playing, the dreams that it weaves, the imagination, the memory; the thousand and one projections that it creates. Watch! Standing there, aloof, distant, not involved, and by and by you will start feeling...

The deeper your watchfulness becomes, the deeper your awareness becomes, gaps start arising, intervals. One thought goes and another has not come, and there is a gap. One cloud has passed, another is coming and there is a gap. In those gaps, for the first time you will have glimpses of no-mind, you will have the taste of no-mind. Call it a taste of Zen, or Tao, or Yoga. In those small intervals, suddenly the sky is clear and the sun is shining. Suddenly the world is full of mystery because all barriers are dropped. The screen on your eyes is no longer there. You see clearly, you see penetratingly. The whole of existence becomes transparent.

In the beginning, there will be just rare moments, few and far between. But they will give you glimpses of what samadhi is. Small pools of silence – they will come and they will disappear. But now you know that you are on the right track – you start watching again.

When a thought passes, you watch it; when an interval passes, you watch it. Clouds are beautiful; sunshine is also beautiful. Now you are not a chooser. Now you don't have a fixed mind: you don't say, "I would like only the intervals." That is stupid – because once you become attached, wanting only the intervals, you have decided again against thinking. And then those intervals will disappear. They happen only when you are very distant, aloof. They happen, they cannot be brought. They happen, you cannot force them to happen. They are spontaneous happenings.

Go on watching. Let thoughts come and go – wherever they want to go. Nothing is wrong! Don't try to manipulate and don't try to direct. Let thoughts move in total freedom. And then bigger intervals will be coming. You will be blessed with mini-satoris. Sometimes minutes will pass and no thought will be there; there will be no traffic – a total silence, undisturbed.

23

DEALING WITH FEELINGS

See the mercury of your emotions rise and fall. Observe when it rises and when it falls. One person vilifies you; another puts a garland around your neck. Observe the fluctuations within. When the abuses and the garlands create no disturbance within and the mercury level remains the same, know then that you are balanced.

EXAGGERATE

For the whole of your life you have been going only so far in everything. If you were angry, you went so far. If you were sad, you went so far. If you were happy, you went so far. There is a subtle line beyond which you have never gone. Everything goes there and stops. It has become almost automatic, so that the moment you reach that line, you are immediately switched off. Everybody has been taught that way: you are allowed a certain anger, but not more than that because more than that can be dangerous. You are allowed a certain happiness, but not more than that because happiness can be maddening. You are allowed sadness only up to a point, but not more than that, because more than that can be suicidal.

You have been trained and there is a Wall of China around you and everybody else. You never go beyond it. That is your only space, your only freedom, so when you start becoming happy, joyous, that Wall of China comes in the way. So you have to be aware of it.

Start doing an experiment that will help tremendously. It is called the method of exaggeration. It is one of the most ancient Tibetan methods of meditation. If you are feeling sad, close your eyes and exaggerate sadness. Go into it as much as possible, go beyond the limit. If you want to moan and sob and weep, do. If you feel like rolling on the floor, do, but go beyond the ordinary limit, where you have never gone.

Exaggerate it because that limit, that constant boundary that you have lived in, has become so much of a routine that unless you go beyond it, you will never be aware – it is part of your habitual mind. So you can become angry, but you will not become aware of it unless you go beyond the boundary. Then suddenly it comes into your awareness because something is happening that has never happened before.

Do this with sadness, with anger, with jealousy, with what-soever you are feeling at the moment – with happiness particu-larly. When you are feeling happy, don't believe in limits. Just go and rush out of the limits: dance, sing, run – don't be a miser. Once you have learned how to trespass the limit, how to tran-scend the limit, you will be in a totally different world. Then you will know how much you have been missing your whole life.

ACCEPT THE CHALLENGE

The only problem with sadness, desperation, anger, hopelessness, anxiety, anguish, misery, is that you want to get rid of them. That's the only barrier.

You will have to live with them. You cannot just escape. They are the very situation in which life has to integrate and grow. They are the challenges of life. Accept them. They are blessings in disguise. If you want to escape from them, if you want somehow to get rid of them, then the problem arises – because if you want to get rid of something, you never look at it directly. And then the thing starts hiding from you because you are condemnatory; then it goes on moving deeper into the unconscious, hides in the darkest corner of your being where you cannot find it. It moves into the basement of your being and hides there. And of course the deeper it goes, the more trouble it creates – because then it starts functioning from unknown corners of your being and you are completely helpless.

So the first thing is: never repress. The first thing is: whatsoever is the case is the case. Accept it and let it come – let it come in front of you. In fact just to say "do not repress" is not enough. If you allow me, I would like to say, "Befriend it." You are feeling sad? Befriend it, have compassion for it. Sadness also has a being. Allow it, embrace it, sit with it, hold hands with it. Be friendly. Be in love with it. Sadness is beautiful. Nothing is wrong with it. Who told you that something is wrong in being sad? In fact only sadness gives you depth. Laughter is shallow; happiness is skin-deep. Sadness goes to the very bones, to the marrow. Nothing goes as deep as sadness.

So don't be worried. Remain with it and sadness will take you to your innermost core. You can ride on it and you will be able to know a few new things about your being that you had never known before. Those things can be revealed only in a sad state; they can never be revealed in a happy state. Darkness is also good and darkness is also divine. Not only the day is God's, the night is his also. I call this attitude religious.

UNDERSTANDING MISERY, PAIN, SUFFERING

It is difficult to get rid of pain, misery, and suffering for the simple reason that they have been your companions for your whole life. Except them, you don't have any friends in the world.

It is easier to be in pain, misery, suffering, than to be utterly lonely because there are ways: you can have painkillers, you can have drugs, as an escape from misery. You can get engaged in all kinds of stupidities to forget your suffering. But there is no way – no painkiller is going to help you out of your loneliness, no drug, no stupidity.

Loneliness is so deep that all these superficial methods cannot reach it, cannot touch it. That's why it is so difficult to get rid of these few friends that you have got. This is your world, your family.

You become addicted to your pain, to your misery, to your suffering. You really don't want to get rid of it. You go on asking how to get rid of it, but that is also a strategy of the mind; to go on inquiring how to get rid of it.

Have you ever sincerely asked if you *want* to get rid of it? Are you ready to live without all the misery and the pain and the suffering that you have been carrying all along? Will you be ready to be left alone without all these longstanding companions who have been with you in thick and thin, who have never left you?

When everybody was leaving you, they were still with you. They have followed you like a shadow; they have been in a certain way a consolation. It will be very shocking to you when I say they have been in a certain way a consolation to you. When I say that, I have many things implied in it.

Your suffering makes you somebody special. Without all your suffering, you are nobody. Who are you? You will not even have something to talk about with anybody. You will be at a loss – what are you going to talk about?

Suffering, misery, pain, are your creations. That is also one of the reasons you cannot get rid of them. You have created them, they are your children. Just look at people when they are talking about their suffering; watch their faces, watch their eyes – and you will be surprised. Are they talking about their suffering or are they bragging about it? Their faces seem radiant when they talk about their suffering. And remember, you know, because you are doing the same. You always exaggerate your pain, your suffering, your misery; you make it as big as possible. Why? If it is something to get rid of, why are you magnifying it? You are enjoying it.

You cannot get rid of your miseries for the simple reason that you don't have anything else to cling to. You will be empty – and nobody wants to be empty. People befool themselves in every possible way.

I have visited areas where people were so hungry – starving; they had no food. I inquired, "You don't have any food, how do you manage to sleep?" Without food you cannot sleep. In fact sleep is needed for one of the most basic things: to digest food. So all other activity is dropped and your whole energy goes into digestion. But when you don't have any food in the stomach, sleep becomes difficult.

I have been fasting, so I know. The night of a fasting day, the whole night you go on tossing and turning, thinking of the next day and of delicious food. And when you are hungry anything looks delicious. But you cannot sleep. I asked, "How do you manage to sleep?"

They said, "We drink a lot of water to fill the belly, to deceive the body, and then sleep comes." They know perfectly well they are deceiving; water is not nourishment. The body is asking for food, and they are giving water because only water is available. But at least something is in the stomach, it is not empty.

This is the situation as far as your psychological emptiness is concerned: anything will do. *Nothing* is not acceptable to you. And unless nothing is acceptable to you, you are not ready to get rid of your pain, misery, and suffering.

The moment you understand, there is no suffering to be thrown out, to be dropped, to be got rid of. Understanding simply cleanses you.

You may have a laugh afterward, but there is no action. You may have a good laugh because you will see how stupid you have been. You have been trying to get rid of things which only need to be understood, and that very understanding becomes freedom from them.

No doing other than understanding is needed.

DROP MISERY

Whenever you have time, whenever you are unoccupied, suddenly the inner hollowness starts opening up and you become afraid. It is like an abyss, you are afraid you may slip into it. Hang onto something, invent something if there is nothing else to hang on to. That's why people are even ready to cling to their misery; nobody is ready to drop his misery easily. That's my experience of working with thousands of people. All their problems can be reduced to one problem: they cling to their misery. It is very difficult for them to drop their miseries because their miseries keep them occupied. Their miseries help them to avoid themselves and their inner hollowness, emptiness, meaninglessness. Their miseries are nothing but a way to escape. Of course those miseries are hurting; hence they talk about how to get rid of them, but they cannot drop them because dropping them means they will be left empty.

So they are in a double bind: they don't want to be miserable and yet they cannot drop their miseries. Miseries are not clinging to you, remember, you are clinging to your miseries.

You can drop your miseries only when some inner meaning starts flowering in you. Miseries can be dropped only when meditation starts blooming in you because then you start enjoying your emptiness, it is no longer empty. Emptiness itself starts having a positive fragrance; it isn't negative anymore. That's the whole magic of meditation: it transforms your emptiness into a positive fulfillment, into something overwhelming. Emptiness becomes silence, emptiness becomes peace; emptiness becomes divine, it becomes godliness.

There is no greater magic than meditation. To transform the negative into the positive, to transform darkness into light, is the miracle of meditation. To transform a trembling person into a fearless soul, to transform a person who was clinging to every stupid thing into a nonclinger, into a nonpossessor, is what happens through meditation.

24

LETTING GO,
DEATH AND DYING

Learn how to dance outwardly, just as a training, as a
discipline, so that the inner dance becomes possible. It is a
mood, a climate – dance is a climate, it has nothing to do with
any activity of dancing. It is a climate, an inner bubbling of
bliss, an inner throbbing of bliss. Only on that boat can the
part that is very, very difficult for you to cross be crossed.
Otherwise one escapes. The moment you face your inner
emptiness you escape, you become scared to death. That's
why so many people never think about themselves. They think
of the whole world, they worry for the whole world, but they
never think about themselves because that point seems to be
touching a wound inside. They are afraid.
Don't be afraid. The existence of things is good; you can profit
by it, but it is not enough. Unless you learn how to be served
by emptiness also, you have not learned the art, the total art.
If you know only how to live, you know only half the art; if you
know also how to die, then you know the whole art – and the
whole art will make you whole.

OSHO NATARAJ MEDITATION
See chapter 8: OSHO Active Meditations

LETTING GO OF THE PAST

You are remembering your past – any happening. Your childhood, your love affairs, the death of your father or mother, anything. Look at it, but don't get involved in it. Remember it as if you are remembering someone else's life. And when this happening is being shown again, is on the screen again, be attentive, aware, a witness, remaining aloof. Your past form will be there in the film, in the story.

If you are remembering your love affair, your first love affair, you will be there with your beloved; your past form will be there with your beloved. Otherwise you cannot remember. Be detached from your past form also. Look at the whole phenomenon as if someone else is loving someone else, as if the whole thing didn't belong to you. You are just a witness, an observer.

COMPLETE THE DAY

When I say to drop the past, I mean that from now onward that is going to be an everyday thing. Every night before you go to sleep, finish that day. It is finished in existence; now it is futile to carry it in the mind. Just be finished with it. Say good-bye to it.

If something has remained incomplete in the day it is difficult to finish it. Complete it, complete it in the mind. You were passing on the road and you saw a beautiful woman and you wanted to hug her. Now that cannot be done; something hangs incomplete. Before you go to sleep just look at the whole day and see what is incomplete. Complete it psychologically: hug her. Relive that moment, hug her in the mind, thank her, and be finished with it. Don't carry it as incomplete. Only incomplete moments are carried. They are hanging because each experience wants to be complete.

There is an intrinsic mechanism in each and everything that compels it to become complete. A seed wants to become the tree, a child wants to become a young man, the unripe fruit wants to become ripe, and so on and so forth. Everything wants to complete itself: it has an inbuilt urge to complete. And that is so about every experience. You wanted to hit somebody and it was not feasible, not practical. It would have cost too much and you were not ready to lose that much. Do it before you go to sleep. Let there be half an hour every night, and that will be your meditation: go on finishing. Start from the morning and finish everything that has remained incomplete. You will be surprised that it can be completed. And once it has been completed you will fall into sleep.

EXPERIENCE DEATH

When a roseflower is disappearing in the evening, its petals are falling, sit there and meditate. Feel yourself as a flower and your petals falling. Early in the morning, when the sun rises and the stars disappear, feel yourself disappearing with all the stars. And when the sun has risen and the dewdrops on the grass leaves start disappearing, feel yourself disappearing like the dewdrops. Feel death in as many ways as possible. Become a great experience of death.

LET DEATH APPEAR LIKE A DEEP REST

Shiva says: *"Focus on fire rising through your form, from the toes up, until the body burns to ashes but not you."*

When you are dying, you cannot inhale. The last act cannot be inhalation; the last act will be exhalation. The first act is inhalation and the last is exhalation. Inhalation is birth and exhalation is death. But every moment you are doing both – inhaling, exhaling. Inhalation is life, exhalation is death.

You may not have observed it, but try to observe. Whenever you exhale, you are more at peace. Exhale deeply and you will feel a certain peace within. Whenever you inhale, you become intense, you become tense. The very intensity of inhalation creates a tension. And the normal, ordinary emphasis is always on inhalation. If I tell you to take deep breaths, you will always start with inhalation. Really, we are afraid of exhaling. That's why breathing has become shallow. You never exhale, you go on inhaling. Only the body goes on exhaling, because the body cannot exist with inhalation alone. It needs both life and death. Try an experiment. The whole day, whenever you remember, exhale deeply and don't inhale. Allow the body to inhale; you simply exhale deeply. And you will feel a deep peace because death is peace, death is silence. And if you can pay attention, more attention, to exhalation, you will feel egoless. With inhalation you will feel more egoistic; with exhalation you will feel more egoless. Pay more attention to exhalation. The whole day, whenever you remember, exhale deeply and don't inhale. Allow the body to inhale; don't do anything.

The emphasis on exhalation will help you very much to do this experiment because you will be ready to die. A readiness is needed, otherwise the technique will not be of much help. And you can be ready only if you have tasted death in a certain way. Exhale deeply and you will have a taste of it. It is beautiful.

Death is just beautiful because nothing is like death – so silent, so relaxing, so calm, so unperturbed. But we are afraid of death. And why are we afraid of death? Why is there so much fear of death? We are not afraid of death because of death – because we don't know it. How can you be afraid of something you have never encountered? How can you be afraid of something that you don't know? At least you must know it to be afraid of it. So really you are not afraid of death; the fear is of something else. You have never really lived – that creates the fear of death.

The fear comes because you are not living, so you are afraid – "I have not lived yet and if death happens, then what? Unfulfilled, unlived, I will die." The fear of death comes only to those who are not really alive. If you are alive, you will welcome death. Then there is no fear. You have known life; now you would like to know death also. But we are so afraid of life itself that we have not known it, we have not entered deeply into it. That creates the fear of death.

If you want to enter this technique, you must be aware of this deep fear. And this deep fear must be thrown away, purged, only then can you enter the technique. This will help: pay more attention to exhalation. And really, if you can pay all your attention to exhalation and forget inhaling... Don't be afraid that you will die; you will not die – the body will inhale by itself. The body has its own wisdom: if you deeply exhale, the body will take a deep inhalation by itself. You need not interfere. Then a very deep relaxation will spread all over your consciousness. The whole day you will feel relaxed and an inner silence will be created.

You can deepen this feeling more if you do another experiment. Just for fifteen minutes in the day exhale deeply. Sit in a chair or on the ground, exhale deeply, and while exhaling, close the eyes. When the air goes out, you go in. Then allow the body to inhale and when the air goes in, open the eyes and you go out. It is just the opposite: when the air goes out, you go in; when the air goes in, you go out.

When you exhale, space is created within because breath is life. When you exhale deeply, you are vacant, life has gone out. In a way you are dead, for a moment you are dead. In that silence of death, enter within. Air is moving out: close your eyes and move within. The space is there and you can move easily.

Before doing the technique, do this for fifteen minutes so that you are ready – not only ready, but welcoming, receptive. The fear of death will not be there because now death appears like a relaxation, death appears like a deep rest.

Death appears not antagonistic to life, but the very source of it, the very energy of it. Life is just like ripples on the face of a lake, and death is the lake itself. When ripples are not there, the lake is there. And the lake can exist without the ripples, but the ripples cannot exist without the lake. Life cannot exist without death. Death can exist without life because it is the source. Then you can do this technique: *Focus on fire rising through your form, from the toes up...*

Just lie down. First conceive of yourself as dead: the body is just like a corpse. Lie down, and then bring your attention to the toes. With closed eyes, move inward. Bring your attention to the toes and feel that the fire is rising from there upward, everything is being burned. As the fire rises, your body is disappearing. Start from the toes and move upward.

Why start from the toes? It will be easier because the toes are very far away from your I, from your ego. Your ego exists in the head. You cannot start from the head, it would be very difficult, so start from the faraway point. The toes are the most faraway point from the ego. Start the fire from there. Feel that the toes are burned, only ashes remain, and then move slowly, burning everything that the fire comes across. Every part – the legs, the thighs – will disappear.

Just go on seeing that they have become ashes. The fire is rising upward, and the parts it has passed are no longer there; they have become ashes. Go on upward, and lastly the head disappears.

Everything has become... The dust has fallen unto dust: ...*until the body burns to ashes but not you.*

You will remain just a watcher on the hill. The body will be there – dead, burned, ashes – and you will be the watcher, you will be the witness. This witness has no ego.

25

THIRD-EYE MEDITATIONS

It is one of the contributions of the East to the world that
between these two eyes, there is a third eye inside which
normally remains dormant.
One has to work hard, bring all the sexual energy upward
against gravity and when the energy reaches the third eye, it
opens. Many methods have been tried to do it because when it
opens there is suddenly a flash of light, and things which have
never been clear to you suddenly become clear.
When I emphasize watching, witnessing, that is the finest
method to bring the third eye into action
because that watching is inside.
These two eyes cannot be used, they can only look outward.
They have to be closed. And when you try to watch inside,
that certainly means there is something like an eye that sees.
Who sees your thoughts? Not these eyes.
Who sees that anger is arising in you?
That point of seeing is symbolically called "the third eye."

OSHO GOURISHANKAR MEDITATION

Osho says that if the breathing is done correctly in the first stage of this meditation, the carbon dioxide formed in the bloodstream will make you feel as high as Gourishankar, Mt Everest. This "high" is carried into the subsequent stages of soft gazing, soft and spontaneous movement, and silent stillness.

This meditation is to be done with its specific OSHO Gourishankar Meditation music, which indicates and energetically supports the different stages. For further details, see Appendix II.

INSTRUCTIONS
The meditation lasts one hour and has four stages.

FIRST STAGE: 15 MINUTES
Sit with closed eyes. Inhale deeply through the nose, filling the lungs. Hold the breath for as long as possible, then exhale gently through the mouth and keep the lungs empty for as long as possible. Continue this breathing cycle throughout the first stage.

SECOND STAGE: 15 MINUTES
Return to normal breathing and with a gentle gaze look at a flashing blue light or a candle flame. Keep your body still.

THIRD STAGE: 15 MINUTES
With closed eyes, stand up and let your body be loose and receptive. The subtle energies will be felt to move the body outside your normal control. Allow this Latihan to happen. Don't do the moving: let moving happen, gently and gracefully.

FOURTH STAGE: 15 MINUTES
Lie down with closed eyes, silent and still.

Note 1: Those with a neurological disorder such as epilepsy should never use a strobe or flashing light for this meditation. Instead they can do the second stage with a blindfold.

Note 2: The music in the second stage of this meditation has a rhythmic beat that is seven times the normal heartbeat. If possible, the flashing light should be a synchronized strobe, at a frequency of 490 per minute. If a strobe light is not possible, you can use a candle.

OSHO MANDALA MEDITATION

Every circle contains a center. In the first three stages of this energetic and powerful technique, centering is the aim, through the creation of a circle of energy. Then, in the fourth stage, the relaxation.

This meditation is to be done with its specific OSHO Mandala Meditation music, which indicates and energetically supports the different stages. For further details, see Appendix II.

INSTRUCTIONS
The meditation lasts one hour and has four stages.

FIRST STAGE: 15 MINUTES
With your eyes open, start running on the spot bringing your knees up as high as possible. Let your breathing be deep and even. Keep going. This will get the energy moving inside.

SECOND STAGE: 15 MINUTES
Sit down with eyes closed, mouth open and loose. Let your body sway from the waist, like a reed blowing in the wind – from side to side, back and forth, around and around, just as it happens.
This will gather your awakened energies at the navel center.

THIRD STAGE: 15 MINUTES
Lie on your back, keeping your head still. Open your eyes and rotate them in a clockwise direction. Sweep them fully around in the sockets, as if you are following the second hand of a vast clock. Start slowly, then gradually turn your eyes faster and faster. Let your mouth remain open and the jaw relaxed, with soft and even breathing. This will bring your centered energies to the third-eye center.

FOURTH STAGE: 15 MINUTES
Close your eyes and be still.

Note: In the first stage there is an alternative for those who find excessive difficulty in jogging. That alternative is "cycling." Lie on your back, with hips on the floor, and rotate your legs as if you are cycling. This can serve as a substitute for jogging.

FINDING THE WITNESS

Shiva says: *"Attention between eyebrows, let mind be before thought. Let form fill with breath essence to the top of the head and there shower as light."* This was the technique given to Pythagoras. Pythagoras went with this technique to Greece and became the fountainhead, the source, of all mysticism in the West. He is the father of all mysticism in the West.

This technique is one of the very deep methods. Try to understand this: *Attention between eyebrows...* Modern physiology, scientific research, says that between the two eyebrows is the gland which is the most mysterious part in the body. This gland, called the pineal gland, is the third eye of the Tibetans – *shiva-netra*: the eye of Shiva, of Tantra. Between the two eyes there exists a nonfunctioning third eye. It is there and can function at any moment, but it is not naturally functioning. You have to do something about it to open it. It is not blind, it is simply closed. This technique is to open the third eye.

Close your eyes and focus both your eyes just in the middle of the two eyebrows. It is as if you are looking with both your eyes. Give your total attention to it.

This is one of the simplest methods of being attentive. You cannot be attentive to any other part of the body so easily. This gland absorbs attention like anything; if you give attention to it, your eyes become hypnotized with the third eye. They become fixed: they cannot move. If you are trying to be attentive to any other part of the body, it is difficult. This third eye catches attention, forces attention. It is magnetic for attention. So all methods all over the world have used it. It is the simplest way to train attention because not only are you trying to be attentive, but the gland itself helps you; it is magnetic. Your attention is forcibly drawn to it. It is absorbed.

Focused at the third eye, suddenly you become a witness. Through the third eye, you become the witness. Through the third eye, you can see thoughts running like clouds in the sky or like people moving on the street.

You are sitting at your window looking at the sky or at people in the street; you are not identified. You are aloof, a watcher on the hill – different. Now if anger is there you can look at it as an object. Now you don't feel that *you* are angry. You feel that you are surrounded by anger – a cloud of anger has come around you – but you are not the anger. And if you are not the anger, the anger becomes impotent, it cannot affect you; you remain untouched. The anger will come and go and you will remain centered in yourself.

When attention is focused at the third-eye center, between the two eyebrows, two things happen. One is that suddenly you become a witness.

This can happen in both directions: become a witness and you will be centered at the third eye... Try to be a witness. Whatsoever is happening, try to be a witness. You are ill, the body is aching and painful, you have misery and suffering, whatsoever: be a witness to it. Whatsoever is happening, don't identify yourself with it. Be a witness – an observer. Then if witnessing becomes possible, you will be focused in the third eye.

Vice versa is also the case: if you are focused in the third eye, you will become a witness. These two things are part of one. So the first thing is that by being centered in the third eye, there will be an arising of the witnessing self. Now you can encounter your thoughts. This will be the first thing.

The second thing will be that now you can feel the subtle, delicate vibration of breathing. Now you can feel the form of breathing, the very essence of breathing.

LOOKING AT THE TIP OF THE NOSE

Lu-tsu says: "*One should look at the tip of one's nose.*"

Why? – because this helps, it brings you in line with the third eye. When both your eyes are fixed on the tip of the nose, it does many things. The basic is that your third eye is exactly in line with the tip of the nose – just a few inches above, but in the same line. And once you are in the line of the third eye, the attraction of the third eye, the pull, the magnetism, of the third eye is so great that you will be pulled even against yourself. You just have to be exactly in line so that the attraction, the gravitation, of the third eye starts functioning. Once you are exactly in line there will be no need for any effort. Suddenly you will find the gestalt has changed because the two eyes create the duality of the world and thought, and the single eye between the two eyes creates the gaps. This is a simple method of changing the gestalt.

One should look at the tip of one's nose. But this does not mean that one should fasten one's thoughts to the tip of the nose. The mind can distort it. The mind can say, "Okay, now look at the tip of the nose. Think of the tip of the nose, concentrate on it." If you concentrate too much on the tip of the nose, you will miss the point because you have to be there at the tip of the nose, but very relaxed so that the third eye can pull you. If you are too concentrated on the tip of the nose, rooted, focused, fixed there, your third eye will not be able to pull you in because your third eye has never functioned before. Its pull cannot be very great in the beginning. Slowly, slowly it grows more and more. Once it starts functioning and the dust that has gathered around it disappears with use, and the mechanism is humming well, then even if you are fixed on the tip of the nose you will be pulled in – but not in the beginning. You have to be very, very light, not a burden, without any stress and strain. You have to be simply there, present, in a kind of let-go.

Lu-tsu says: *"Only when the eyelids are lowered properly halfway is the tip of the nose seen in just the right way. Therefore it is taken as a guideline. The main thing is to lower the eyelids in the right way, and then to allow the light to stream in of itself."*

That is very important to remember: you are not to pull the light in, you are not to force the light in. If the window is open, the light comes in of its own accord. If the door is open, the light floods in. You need not bring it in, you need not push it in, you need not drag it in. And how can you drag light in? How can you push light in? All that is needed is that you should be open and vulnerable to it.

And that's exactly what happens when you are looking at the tip of the nose. Just looking, without any concentration; just looking, without any heaviness in it, without any strain in it, suddenly the window of the third eye opens and the light starts streaming in. The light that has always been going out starts coming in too and the circle is complete.

This circle makes a man perfect. And this circle makes a man utterly restful, relaxed. This circle makes a man whole and holy. He is no longer divided.

26

JUST SITTING

You are simply sitting there doing nothing.
All is silence and all is peace and all is bliss.
You have entered godliness, you have entered truth.

ZAZEN

INSTRUCTIONS

Sit comfortably facing a plain wall approximately an arm's length away. The eyes should be half-open, allowing the gaze to rest softly on the wall. Alternatively, you can sit facing a garden or the sky – any place with not much movement. Keep your back straight and rest one hand inside the other with thumbs touching to form an oval. Stay as still as possible for 30 minutes. You can follow this with a short walking meditation and then repeat the sitting, as you like.

While sitting, allow a choiceless awareness, not directing the attention anywhere in particular, but remaining as receptive and alert as possible, moment to moment.

Zen people say: "Just sit, don't do anything." The most difficult thing in the world is just to sit doing nothing. But once you have got the knack of it... If you go on for a few months, sitting doing nothing for a few hours every day, slowly, slowly many things will happen. You will feel sleepy, you will dream. Many thoughts will crowd your mind, many things. The mind will say, "Why are you wasting your time? You could have earned a little money. At least you could have gone to a film, entertained yourself, or you could have relaxed and gossiped. You could have watched TV or listened to the radio, or at least you could have read the newspaper you have not seen. Why are you wasting your time?"

The mind will give you a thousand and one arguments, but if you just go on listening without being bothered by the mind... It will do all kinds of tricks: it will hallucinate, it will dream, it will become sleepy. It will do all that is possible to drag you out of just sitting. But if you go on, if you persevere, one day the sun rises.

One day it happens: you are not feeling sleepy, the mind has become tired of you, is fed up with you, has dropped the idea that you can be trapped, is simply finished with you! There is no sleep, no hallucination, no dream, no thought. You are simply sitting there doing nothing. And all is silence and all is peace and all is bliss. You have entered godliness, you have entered truth.

⁓

You can sit anywhere, but whatsoever you are looking at should not be too exciting. For example, things should not be moving too much. They become a distraction. You can watch the trees – that is not a problem because they are not moving and the scene remains constant. You can watch the sky or just sit in the corner watching the wall.

The second thing is, don't look at anything in particular – just emptiness, because the eyes are there and one has to look at something, but you are not looking at anything in particular. Don't focus or concentrate on anything – just a diffuse image. That relaxes very much.

And the third thing is, relax your breathing. Don't do it, let it happen. Let it be natural and that will relax even more.

The fourth thing is, let your body remain as immobile as possible. First find a good posture – you can sit on a pillow or mattress or whatever you feel to, but once you settle, remain immobile because if the body does not move, the mind automatically falls silent. In a moving body, the mind also continues to move, because bodymind are not two things. They are one: it is one energy.

In the beginning it will seem a little difficult, but after a few days you will enjoy it tremendously. You will see, by and by, layer upon layer of the mind starting to drop. A moment comes when you are simply there with no mind.

SITTING SILENTLY
FOR NO REASON AT ALL

One has to learn not to be so concerned with the result, with the goal. One should start enjoying the journey itself. One should start enjoying the trees by the side of the road, the birds singing, the sun rising, the clouds floating in the sky. One should move slowly, at one's natural pace. And one should not even be in competition with others because everybody has their own natural pace and everybody has a unique individuality.

So, one should listen to one's own heart. And it is not difficult to judge: if you are in a hurry, you are tense. That tension is enough to indicate, it is an indicator that you are doing something against your nature, you are straining too much. Slow down. Move in a relaxed way, as if the whole of infinity is available. In fact it is so, the whole of infinity *is* available. We are not born with our birth and we don't die with our death either. We are eternal. One can go into deep meditation only with this understanding. One should forget completely whether anything is happening or not. One should start enjoying just sitting silently, for no reason at all, with no motive at all – just for the sheer joy of sitting silently, just breathing, being, listening to the birds or watching your breath. Slowly, slowly a new fragrance starts arising in your being. That fragrance is meditation, that poise, that calmness, that stillness. It comes from the beyond as a gift. And whenever someone is ready it always happens, inevitably.

SITTING IN A BUS OR TRAIN

You are using awareness without being aware of it, but only about outside things. It is the same awareness that has to be used for the inside traffic. When you close your eyes, there is a traffic of thoughts, emotions, dreams, imaginations – all kinds of things start flashing by.

What you have been doing with the outside world, do exactly the same with the inside world and you will become a witness. And once tasted, the joy of being a witness is so great, so otherworldly, that you would like to go in more and more. Whenever you find time you would like to go in more and more.

And it is not a question of any posture; it is not a question of any temple, of any church or synagogue. When you have nothing to do sitting in a public bus or in a train, just close your eyes. It will save your eyes becoming tired from looking outside, and it will give you time enough to watch yourself. Those moments will become moments of the most beautiful experiences.

27

LAUGHTER AS MEDITATION

Learn to laugh. Seriousness is a sin and a disease.
Laughter has tremendous beauty, lightness.
It will bring lightness to you and it will give you wings to fly.
Life is so full of opportunities; you just need the sensitivity.
And create chances for other people to laugh.
Laughter should be one of the most valued, cherished qualities
of human beings.

OSHO LAUGHTER MEDITATION

This meditation helps you to start enjoying the small things of life – childlike, liquid, mirrorlike. The first stage is of giggling and laughing, in the second stage you earth yourself; energized by this, your dance in the last stage will have a different quality.

This meditation can be done with its specific OSHO Laughter Meditation recording, which indicates and energetically supports the different stages. For further details, see Appendix II.

INSTRUCTIONS
The meditation lasts one hour and has three stages. Stay in your own space throughout, with no interaction.

FIRST STAGE: 20 MINUTES
Sitting silently, eyes closed, create a giggle in the very guts of your being, as if your whole body is giggling and laughing. Start swaying with the laughter and let it spread from the belly to the whole of your body: hands laughing, feet laughing.
Go crazily into it. If it comes uproariously, loudly, allow it; if it comes silently, then sometimes silently, sometimes loudly – but keep on laughing.

SECOND STAGE: 20 MINUTES
Lie down, spread yourself on the floor, facing the floor. Make contact with the earth, the whole body lying there, and just feel that the earth is the mother and you are the child. Get lost in that feeling. Breathe with the earth, feel one with the earth.

THIRD STAGE: 20 MINUTES
Stand up and start dancing. Energized by the earthing, you will have so much energy that your dancing will have a different quality to it. Just dance, any dance.

If it is warm and you can do it in the garden, on the soil, that will be far better; if it can be done naked, that will be even better. Make contact with the earth, the whole body lying down there on the earth. We come from the earth and one day we will be going back to it. After the twenty minutes energizing, dance for twenty minutes, just any dance – the earth will have given so much energy that your dancing will have a different quality to it; put music on and dance.

If it is difficult, it is cold, then you can do this inside a room; when it is sunny, do it outside. If it is very cold, cover yourself with a blanket. Find ways and means but continue to do it.

OSHO MYSTIC ROSE
See chapter 11: OSHO Meditative Therapies

WAKE UP, STRETCH, AND LAUGH

In the morning when you feel sleep has left you, don't open your eyes immediately. The mind has a tendency to open the eyes immediately. You miss a great opportunity because when sleep leaves you and life energies are wakening inside, you can watch them, and that watching will be very helpful for going into deeper meditation.

The mind is fresh, the body is fresh after the whole night's rest; everything is fresh, unburdened. There is no dust, no tired-ness – you can look deeply, penetratingly. Your eyes are fresher; everything is vital. Don't miss that moment. When you feel sleep has left, don't open the eyes immediately. Remain with closed eyes and feel the energy which is changing now from sleep to waking. And that's what I am going to teach you: how to change all your energies from sleep to waking. So just watch.

You may be lethargic in that moment, you would like to turn over and go to sleep again, so for three minutes with closed eyes stretch your body like a cat. But with closed eyes: don't open the eyes and don't look at the body from without. Look at the body from within. Stretch, move, let the body energy flow, and feel it. When it is fresh it is good to feel it; the feeling will remain with you the whole day.

Do this for two or three minutes – if you enjoy it, five min-utes. And then for two or three minutes laugh loudly like a mad-man, but with closed eyes. Don't open the eyes: laugh loudly with closed eyes. The energies are there, flowing; the body is awake and alert and vital. The sleep has gone. You are filled, flooded with new energy.

The first thing to be done is laughter because it sets the trend for the whole day. If you do it, you will feel within two or three days that for the whole day your mood remains one of laughing, enjoying.

JUST START LAUGHING

Laughter needs a great learning, and laughter is a great medicine. It can cure many of your tensions, anxieties, worries; all the energy can flow into laughter.

And there is no need for there to be some occasion, some cause. In my meditation camps I used to have a laughing meditation – people would sit and just start laughing for no reason. At first they would feel a little awkward that there was no reason, but when everybody was doing it, they would also start. Soon, everybody was in such a great laughter, people were rolling on the ground. They were laughing at the very fact that so many people were laughing for no reason at all; there was nothing, not even a joke had been told. And it went on like waves.

So there is no harm. Even just sitting in your room, close the doors and have an hour of simple laughter.

HAVE A GOOD LAUGH

The moment you feel you are serious, laugh about it and see where the seriousness is. Laugh, give a good laugh, close the eyes and look where it is. You will not find it. It exists only in a being who cannot laugh.

A more unfortunate situation cannot be conceived, a poorer being cannot be conceived of, than the man who cannot laugh at himself. So start the morning by laughing at yourself, and whenever you can find a moment in the day when you have nothing to do, have a good laugh for no particular reason – just because the whole world is so absurd, just because the way you are is so absurd. There is no need to find any particular reason. The whole thing is such that one has to laugh.

Let the laughter be belly laughter, not a heady thing. One can laugh from the head – then it is dead. From the head everything is dead; the head is absolutely mechanical. You can laugh from the head, then your head will create the laughter, but it will not go deep in the belly to the *hara*. It will not go to your toes, it will not go to your whole body.

A real laughter has to be just like a small child laughs. Watch his belly shaking, his whole body throbbing with it. He wants to roll on the floor – it is a question of totality. He laughs so much that he starts crying; he laughs so deeply that the laughter hits his tears, tears come out of him. Laughter should be deep and total. This is the medicine that I prescribe for seriousness.

28

MAKE SLEEP A MEDITATION

At night Buddha slept only on one side. Ananda asked him
one day, "Whenever I get up at night you are always
sleeping on the same side. Even your hands don't move, they
also remain in the same position. Do you sleep consciously?
Don't you relax in your sleep?"
Buddha replied, "One who is awake doesn't sleep. One has to
sleep consciously. I sleep, but someone within me is always
awake because if there is no wakefulness within, then
dreaming starts. And if dreaming goes on inside, thoughts will
go on during the daytime. If one is not awake at night, then
it is difficult to be awake even during the daytime. Waking
should be natural all the time – day and night. The inner flow
of wakefulness should continue."
So even at night Buddha slept consciously, he kept his hands
in the same position. He didn't let unconsciousness come in,
even in his sleep.

SLIP INTO SLEEP MEDITATIVELY

There is a story about Gautam Buddha. Every night his disciples had to meditate before going to sleep. And it was a very significant thing because if you can go into sleep with a silent, peaceful mind, that space of silence and peace is carried all through your night. Just one hour of meditation before sleep turns into eight hours of meditation.

Whatever is your last thought when you fall asleep will be your first thought when you wake up. You can check it: just remember what your last thought is and you will be amazed – as you start feeling that you are awakening, the same thought is standing at your door.

It means you can use six or eight hours of sleep in a tremendously creative way. And the most significant will be to go into sleep, slip into sleep, meditatively. Meditation slowly, slowly becomes your sleep, and then your sleep becomes meditation. And to meditate eight hours or six hours is going to change you so totally, without any effort, that you will be surprised: you have not done anything, but now you are not the same person who used to be angry over small things, who used to hate, who used to be greedy, who used to be violent, who used to be jealous, who used to be competitive.

All those things have disappeared and you have not done anything – you have simply been meditating before you go to sleep. That is the best time because in the day you cannot get six hours to devote to meditation. But anyway you sleep – why not transform your sleep into meditation? That was a great contribution of Gautam Buddha.

WATCH SLEEP COME AND GO

Meditation has to be just watchfulness, then it is possible to have it twenty-four hours a day. Even while going to sleep, be watchful. To the last moment, when you see that now sleep is taking over – the darkness goes on growing, the body is relaxing and the point comes when suddenly from wakefulness you move into sleep – watch up to that moment. And first thing in the morning, as you become aware that the sleep is finished, immediately start watching; soon you will be able to watch even while you are asleep. Watchfulness will become a lamp that goes on burning day and night inside you.

This is the only authentic meditation. All else that has been told to you in the name of meditation is simply a toy to play with, to deceive yourself that you are doing something spiritual. With this meditation you will come across the inescapable. Everything illusory will disappear.

SLEEPING FULLY AWARE

My meditation is not something separate from life, it is something that has to be spread all over life. Your whole life has to be colored by it. So whatever you do – you make love, but meditation remains. You cannot drop it even while making love. It is not like your glasses, you cannot take it off! It is like eyes, they are always there. You cannot just take them off and put them on again.

My meditation is a method of being aware of whatever you are doing, thinking, feeling. You have to become aware on all three layers. A time comes when even when you are going to sleep... Even then, while you are sitting on the bed, sit in awareness, lie down in awareness. Wait for sleep, fully watchful: when it comes, how it comes, how slowly it descends on you, how your body starts relaxing, in which points there was tension, and now the tension is gone.

A day will come, it certainly comes, when the body will have gone to sleep and your meditation will still be there like a flame inside you, burning, fully aware. This is the moment that I call your meditation complete. Now you can meditate even in sleep. So there is no question: while awake you will be able to meditate, there is no problem.

And the man who can meditate in sleep will be able to meditate while dying because the process is the same. Just as in sleep you slowly, slowly go deeper inside you – the body is left far away, relaxed, the mind slows down, the thoughts go on disappearing – exactly the same happens in death. A man who knows meditation never dies. He remains alive, aware. Death is happening, he is there.

IF YOU SUFFER FROM INSOMNIA

Note: This meditation is an adaptation of The Heart of Peacefulness (see chapter 14: Heart Meditations,) where the technique is to "Close your eyes and just feel the area between the armpits: the heart area, your chest. First feel it, just between the armpits, and bring your total attention, total awareness. Forget the whole body, just the heart area between the armpits, the chest, and feel it filled with great peace."

Try this. And whenever you are able to feel the peace between your armpits filling you, pervading your heart center, the world will look illusory. When the world feels and appears to be illusory, that is a sign that you have entered meditation. Don't *think* that the world is illusory, there is no need to think it – you will feel it. It will suddenly come to your mind, "What has happened to the world?" The world will have suddenly gone dreamy. It is there, but without any substance, just like a film on a screen. It can even be three-dimensional. It looks so real, like something that has been projected. It is not that the world is a projected thing, not that it is really unreal – no. The world is real but you create a distance, and the distance becomes more and more. You can know whether the distance is becoming more and more, or not, by seeing how you feel about the world. That's the criterion. It is not a truth that the world is unreal; that is a meditative criterion – if the world has become unreal, you have become centered in the being. Now the surface and you are so far apart that you can look at the surface as something objective, something other than you. You are not identified.

This technique is very easy and will not take much time if you try it. It sometimes even happens with this technique that you will feel the beauty and the miracle of it on your very first effort.

Do it for ten minutes at night, just before falling asleep. Make the world unreal, and your sleep will be so deep that you may not have slept like that before. If the world becomes unreal just before falling asleep, the dreams will be fewer because if the world has become a dream, then dreams cannot continue. And if the world is unreal, you are totally relaxed because the reality of the world will not impinge itself upon you, hammer on you. I have suggested this technique to people who suffer from insomnia. It helps deeply. If the world is unreal, tensions dissolve. And if you can move from the periphery, you have already moved to a deep state of sleep – before sleep comes, you are already deeply into it. Then in the morning it is beautiful because you are so fresh, so young; all the energy is vibrating, coming from the center back to the periphery.

FORGET ABOUT SLEEP

Try one night to go to sleep, make an effort to go to sleep, and it will become more and more impossible for you. Every night you go to sleep very easily. If you want to suffer from insomnia this is a sure method to suffer from insomnia. Try, make an effort to go to sleep. Toss and turn and take long breaths and count sheep and jog in the room and take a bath and do some Transcendental Meditation. And then naturally sleep will become impossible, because all these things will be disturbances, distractions. How do you go to sleep? If somebody asks you, will you ever be able to explain? How do you manage? Every night when you fall asleep you are doing a miracle. You are moving from doing to nondoing, from action to no-action. How do you manage it? Is there any art? Have you learned it? What is the trick in it? Try to think about it, and then you will never be able to sleep.

If somebody asks you how you go to sleep, don't try to find the answer, otherwise you will suffer from insomnia from that very day. People who suffer from insomnia just need to forget about sleep; there is no need to worry about it. If you are not feeling sleepy, be happy, enjoy, read something, listen to music, sing, dance, go for a walk. You are more fortunate than the people who are fast asleep and snoring. But forget all about sleep. Watch the stars, enjoy the stars, feel yourself far more fortunate than the others, and you will fall asleep without any effort on your part. But don't make any effort.

29

ANYTHING CAN BE
A MEDITATION

If we can de-automatize our activities, then the whole of life
becomes a meditation. Then any small thing, taking a shower,
eating your food, talking to your friend, becomes meditation.
Meditation is a quality; it can be brought to anything. It is not
a specific act. People think that way, they think meditation is
a specific act: when you sit facing the east, you repeat certain
mantras, you burn incense, you do this and that at a particular
time in a particular way with a particular gesture. Meditation
has nothing to do with all those things. They are all ways to
automatize and meditation is against automatization.
So if you can keep alert, any activity is meditation.

PHYSICAL WORK OR EXERCISE

For a meditator, physical work has great significance and use-fulness – not because you will produce something out of it but because the more you are involved in some kind of labor, the more your consciousness will start becoming centered. It will start coming downward from the mind. It is not necessary for the labor to be productive. It can be nonproductive also, it can be simple exercise. But some physical labor is absolutely essen-tial for the agility of the body, the complete alertness of the mind and the total awakening of the being.

RUNNING, JOGGING, AND SWIMMING

It is natural and easy to keep alert while you are in movement. When you are just sitting silently, the natural thing is to just fall asleep. When you are lying on your bed it is very difficult to keep alert because the whole situation helps you fall asleep. But in movement you naturally cannot fall asleep, you function in a more alert way. The only problem is that the movement can become mechanical.

Learn to melt your body, mind, soul: find ways you can func-tion as a unity.

It happens many times that runners... You would not think of running as a meditation, but runners have sometimes had a tremendous experience of meditation. And they were surprised because they were not looking for it – who thinks that a run-ner is going to experience godliness? But it has happened, and now running is more and more becoming a new kind of medi-tation. It can happen in running. If you have ever been a run-ner, if you have enjoyed running in the early morning when the air is fresh and young and the whole world is coming back out of sleep, awakening, and you were running and your body was functioning beautifully, and the fresh air, and the new world again born out of the darkness of the night, and everything singing all around, and you were feeling so alive... A moment comes when the runner disappears, there is only running. The body, mind, and soul start functioning together; suddenly an inner orgasm is released.

Runners have sometimes come accidentally on the experience of the fourth, *turiya*, although they will miss it because they will think it was just because of running that they enjoyed the moment: that it was a beautiful day, that the body was healthy and the world was beautiful, and it was just a certain mood. They will not take note of it. But if they do take note of it, my own observation is that a runner can more easily come close to meditation than anybody else. Jogging can be of immense help, swimming can be of immense help. All these things have to be transformed into meditations.

Start running in the morning on the road. Start with half a mile and then one mile and come eventually to at least three miles. While running use the whole body; don't run as if you are in a straitjacket. Run like a small child, using the whole body – hands and feet – and run. Breathe deeply and from the belly. Then sit under a tree, rest, perspire and let the cool breeze come; feel peaceful. This will help very deeply.

Never become an expert in running; remain an amateur so that alertness is kept. If you feel sometimes that running has become automatic, drop it; try swimming. If that becomes automatic, then try dancing. The point to remember is that the movement is just a situation to create awareness. While it creates awareness it is good. If it stops creating awareness, then it is no longer of any use; change to another movement where you will have to be alert again. Never allow any activity to become automatic.

JUST STAND ON THE EARTH

Sometimes just stand on the earth without shoes and feel the coolness, the softness, the warmth. Whatsoever the earth is ready to give in that moment, just feel it and let it flow through you. And allow your energy to flow into the earth. Be connected with the earth.

If you are connected with the earth, you are connected with life. If you are connected with the earth, you are connected with your body. If you are connected with the earth, you will become very sensitive and centered – and that's what is needed.

WHEN EATING, EAT

If you are eating, let your whole consciousness be that of taste, of smell. Forget everything. Then even ordinary bread may taste like the most delicious food possible. But you are not present…

Look at people eating – they are talking, there are people who are listening to the radio or watching TV. I have heard about stupid Americans even making love while watching TV! What to say about eating? Why miss? You can do both things; you can make love and you can go on watching TV. Now, neither you will be watching TV nor will you be making love; you will not be able to enjoy either, you will miss both. There are people who cannot eat if they don't have company, to talk and gossip and discuss. When you are talking you just go on swallowing – swallowing is not eating.

Eating should be meditative, prayerful. You should be more respectful to food because it is life, it is nourishment. And then a thousand and one problems arise out of it. While you are eating and you are reading the newspaper or quarreling with the wife or listening to the radio or watching TV or talking to a friend or holding the phone, you will miss the joy of eating. You will eat more because your taste buds will not feel fulfilled and contented. You will gather unnecessary fat in the body. Then one has to start dieting, fasting, naturopathy – and all kinds of nonsense follow. But the simple thing that should have been done in the first place was: just eating and not doing anything else.

SMOKING

A man came to me. He had been suffering from chain-smoking for thirty years; he was ill and the doctors said, "You will never be healthy if you don't stop smoking." But he was a chronic smoker; he could not help it. He had tried – not that he had not tried – he had tried hard and had suffered much in trying, but only for one day or two days, and then again the urge would come so tremendously, it would simply take him away. Again he would fall into the same pattern.

Because of this smoking he had lost all self-confidence: he knew he could not do a small thing: he could not stop smoking. He had become worthless in his own eyes; he thought himself just the most worthless person in the world. He had no respect for himself.

He came to me and asked, "What can I do? How can I stop smoking?"

I said, "Nobody can stop smoking. You have to understand. Smoking is not only a question of your decision now. It has entered your world of habits; it has taken roots. Thirty years is a long time. It has taken roots in your body, in your chemistry; it has spread all over. It is not just a question of your head deciding; your head cannot do anything. The head is impotent: it can start things, but it cannot stop them so easily. Once you have started and practiced so long, you are a great yogi – thirty years practicing smoking! It has become automatic; you will have to de-automatize it."

He asked, "What do you mean by 'de-automatization'?"

And that's what meditation is all about: de-automatization.

I said, "Do one thing: forget about stopping. There is no need either. For thirty years you have smoked and lived; of course it was a suffering but you have become accustomed to that too. And what does it matter if you die a few hours earlier than you would have died without smoking? What are you going to do here? What have you done? So what is the point – whether you die Monday or Tuesday or Sunday, this year, that year – what does it matter?"

He said, "Yes, that is true, it doesn't matter."

Then I said, "Forget about it; we are not going to stop it at all. Rather, we are going to understand it. So next time, make it a meditation."

He said, "A meditation out of smoking?"

I said, "Yes. If Zen people can make a meditation out of

drinking tea and can make it a ceremony, why not? Smoking can be as beautiful a meditation."

He looked thrilled. He said, "What are you saying?"

He became alive! He said, "A meditation? Just tell me – I can't wait!"

I gave him the meditation. I said, "Do one thing. When you are taking the packet of cigarettes out of your pocket, move slowly. Enjoy it, there is no hurry. Be conscious, alert, aware; take it out slowly with full awareness. Then take the cigarette out of the packet with full awareness, slowly – not in the old hurried way, the unconscious, mechanical way. Then start tapping the cigarette on your packet – but very alertly. Listen to the sound, just as Zen people do when the samovar starts singing and the tea starts boiling. And the aroma… Then smell the cigarette and the beauty of it…"

He said, "What are you saying? The beauty?"

"Yes, it is beautiful. Tobacco is as divine as anything. Smell it; it is God's smell."

He looked a little surprised. He said, "What! Are you joking?"

"No, I am not joking. Even when I joke, I don't joke. I am very serious. Then put it in your mouth, with full awareness, light it with full awareness. Enjoy every act, every small act, and divide it into as many acts as possible, so you can become more and more aware.

"Then have the first puff: God in the form of smoke. Hindus say, 'Annam brahman – food is God.' Why not smoke? All is God. Fill your lungs deeply – this is a pranayam. I am giving you the new Yoga for the new age! Then release the smoke, relax, another puff – and go very slowly.

"If you can do it, you will be surprised; soon you will see the whole stupidity of it. Not because others have said that it is stupid, not because others have said that it is bad. You will see it. And the seeing will not just be intellectual. It will be from your total being; it will be a vision of your totality. And then one day, if it drops, it drops; if it continues, it continues. You need not worry about it."

After three months he came and he said, "It dropped."

"Now," I said, "try it on other things too."

This is the secret, *the* secret: de-automatize. Walking, walk slowly, watchfully. Looking, look watchfully, and you will see trees are greener than they have ever been and roses are rosier than they have ever been. Listen. Somebody is talking, gossiping: listen, listen attentively. When you are talking, talk attentively. Let all your waking activity become de-automatized.

BRING JOY TO EVERY ACT

Remain cheerful, like the birds are cheerful in the early morning. Let there always be a song on inside you, a constant humming. It has to become an undercurrent. Go on doing whatsoever you are doing, but let there be a constant undercurrent of cheerfulness. Everything else will change, but don't let your cheerfulness change. Even if sometimes on the surface you are feeling sad, depressed, don't forget that deep underneath there is a current where you are still cheerful, still blissful.

Slowly, slowly that awareness transforms one's whole being. Sadness simply disappears, the negative is not found at all, and with the negative, the positive also disappears. Then real cheerfulness arises. Then there is nobody who is cheerful but only a state of cheerfulness. You cannot call it positive because there is never anything opposed to it. It simply is, neither this nor that; it simply is. That isness is God, and there is no other God except that; all other Gods are inventions of man.

Seek and search bliss, and one need not go anywhere else. One has to create an inner discipline. So if you are cooking food you can go on cooking food, but let there be a song, a humming; cooking has to become a play. If you are cleaning the floor, go on cleaning, but why not hum, why not remain in an inner rhythm? Bring joy to every act and every activity.

30

CHILDREN AND MEDITATION

Meditation is a way to go within yourself to that depth where
thoughts don't exist, so it is not indoctrination. It is not
teaching you anything, in fact, it is just making you alert to
your inner capacity to be without thought, to be without mind.
And the best time is when a child is still uncorrupted.

PLAY MEDITATION

Children can go into meditation very easily – one just has to know how to help them toward it. They cannot be coerced; that's impossible. Nobody can ever be coerced into meditation because coercion is violence. How can one coerce meditation? It comes when it comes. But you can persuade.

You can just invite the child with tremendous respect. Dance with him, sing with him, sit in silence with him. By and by he will start imbibing it. By and by he will start enjoying the play of it.

It cannot be a work for him. It cannot be a serious thing for him – it should not be for anybody. It can only be a play. So help him to play meditation. Let it be a game. Make it a game with him, and by and by he will start loving it. He will start asking you, "When are we going to play meditation?" And once he starts learning ways of silence, then meditation has started working on him, and one day you will see that he is deeper in meditation than you had ever expected. So you have to make a meditative atmosphere.

You have just to persuade him toward meditativeness. It has nothing to do with any ideology – Christian, Hindu, Mohammedan; they are all irrelevant. It is more like love; it is a feeling. And if he can learn something of it, then it starts growing on its own. One day he will be grateful for it, grateful that you helped him. Right now he cannot understand, so the whole responsibility is yours.

It is my observation that if grown-ups are a little more meditative, children imbibe the spirit very easily. They are so sensitive. They learn whatsoever is there in the atmosphere; they learn the vibe of it.

BE NOISY, THEN BE SILENT

Osho,
My six- and seven-year-old children at school sometimes
like to make noise and run and I do not want to force them
to stay in place and be silent.

Do one thing: every day, at least twice, give them fifteen or twenty minutes to go berserk, to go completely mad and do whatsoever they want to do – to jump and scream and shout. Just twenty minutes in the morning before you start your class. You also participate, then they will enjoy it very much – also shout and jump and participate, then they will be really into it. The moment they see that their teacher is into it, they will simply enjoy the whole trip. Just fifteen minutes will do. Tell them to be as noisy as they can and do whatsoever they want to do. Then tell them to stop and for five minutes remain silent; this will be a great meditation to them.

And if you feel it works, then once more somewhere in the afternoon before they leave, do it again. Within two or three months you will see such a change coming to the children... Unbelievable...

Their pent-up energy has to be released. In fact they have so much energy and we are forcing them to sit and they cannot, so they are boiling! They find any chance and they will start doing mischief. Just allow them, try it. It will be a great help, and you will see: they will become more intelligent, their concentration will become better, their capacity to hear will become better, their understanding will become better, because they will be no longer burdened.

FROM GIBBERISH TO SILENCE

This is a meditation that leaves the mind more pure and fresh. Children and teachers can try it together and it can also be done at home – but it should not be made compulsory.

Osho suggested this meditation when a schoolteacher asked for a meditation suitable for children. It has three stages for children below twelve years, and four stages for those who are twelve and over.

INSTRUCTIONS
You can choose whether to do the meditation with each stage lasting 5 minutes or with each stage lasting 10 minutes.

FIRST STAGE:
*Gibberish. Make nonsense sounds and speak any language you
don't know. You have total freedom to shout, scream, and express
your feelings.*

SECOND STAGE:
Laughing. You are allowed to laugh totally, for no reason at all.

LAST STAGE:
*Lie down – still and silent as if you are dead, only the breathing
comes and goes.*

Note: The following is the extra stage for those twelve years or older.

THIRD STAGE:
Cry and weep without any reason, to your heart's content.

FEEL LIKE A TREE AND SWAY

*Osho,
I am twelve years old; can I start meditating?*

This is the right age when you should start meditating, just
when you are coming closer to your fourteenth year. You are
twelve; these two years will be of immense value to you. After
each seven years the mind changes. The fourteenth year will
be one of great change, so if one is ready, much becomes possible; if one is not ready, then one goes on missing the change.
And all that is beautiful always happens when you are passing
that period of change. At seven the childhood disappears; at
fourteen the adolescence is gone; and then at twenty-one and
at twenty-eight things go on changing. Each seven years there
is a cycle.

So start meditating. And by meditation I mean that whenever you are sitting silently, start swaying... Feel like a tree and
sway. As you sway and as you feel like a tree, you will disappear as a human being and in that disappearance is meditation.
There are a thousand and one ways to disappear. I am giving

you the simplest, one that you can do very easily. Dance, and disappear into the dance; whirl, and disappear into the whirl. Jog, run, and disappear into the jogging: let the jogging be there and forget about yourself. That forgetfulness is meditation, and that is possible at this age.

Then there are different doors to meditation which become possible later on, but to a child, forgetfulness is meditation. So forget yourself in anything and you will find meditation coming to you.

OSHO NATARAJ MEDITATION
See chapter 8: OSHO Active Meditations

Children can enter meditation through dance very easily because dance is not something unnatural, artificial; man is born with the facility of dance. Because we have stopped dancing naturally, the body is suffering very much. There are a few things that can happen only through dance: flow is possible only through dance. So help your child to participate in dancing meditations. If she can get into dance, meditation will happen of its own accord.

APPENDIX I: INDEX OF MEDITATIONS

APPENDIX II: ONLINE RESOURCES AND RECOMMENDED READING

YOUR MOST IMPORTANT WEB LINKS

The meditation music and other support materials mentioned in this book are available from a variety of publishers and distributors throughout the world.
*Many of these are listed on **www.osho.com/shop**.*
*Also see **www.osho.com/allaboutosho** and **imeditate.osho.com**.*

OSHO Active Meditations

Much of the music to support the OSHO Active Meditations has been composed under Osho's direction, and with his instruction that once finalized, the music should remain the same, not be changed in any way. The music for each particular meditation was composed uniquely for that meditation.
Audio and video instructions for the OSHO Active Meditations and other OSHO Meditations are given on osho.com/meditation and on imeditate.osho.com. For live participation options from your home, log in on: imeditate.osho.com.

OSHO Reminding Yourself of the Forgotten Language of Talking to Your BodyMind

Music with voice to accompany this process has been published in many languages.

OSHO Talks: Silence Shared in Words

Almost all of the OSHO Talk series have been published in full as books. Audio recordings of each individual talk are available and additionally a selection of OSHO Talks is available in video format.

OSHO Evening Meeting Meditation

Besides gathering the materials for the individual components of the OSHO Evening Meeting Meditation, you can also log in for live participation on imeditate.osho.com.

RECOMMENDED OSHO BOOKS

Osho books are available in at least 50 languages. Here are some of the English titles we recommend specifically on the subject of meditation, for your further reading:

The Book of Secrets
112 Meditations to Discover the Mystery Within
Osho describes each method from as many angles as possible and suggests that if you feel any affinity with it, to play with it for three days. If you feel that it fits, that something clicks in you, continue it for three months.

Pharmacy for the Soul
A Collection of OSHO Meditations, Relaxation and Awareness Exercises, and Other Practices for Physical and Emotional Well-Being
This is a selection of awareness and meditation methods, taken from Osho's many individual talks with people from around the world. They include meditations, laughter and breathing exercises, vocalizations, visualizations, chants and more.

Learning to Silence the Mind
Wellness through Meditation
The mind, says Osho, has the potential to be enormously creative in dealing with the challenges of everyday life. If only there was a way to switch it off and give it a rest! Finding the switch that can silence the mind through understanding, watchfulness, and a healthy sense of humor – is meditation.

Body Mind Balancing
Using Your Mind to Heal Your Body
This book is of great help in learning to talk to, listen to, and reconnect with our bodies, and in deeply grasping the unity of body, mind and being. An awareness of the body, says Osho, is the easiest starting point.
The guided OSHO Meditative Therapy and relaxation process, "OSHO Reminding Yourself of the Forgotten Language of Talking to Your BodyMind" is an audio CD that accompanies the book.

From Medication to Meditation
How Meditation Supports Physical and Psychological Health

Osho requested and titled this collection of insights into what makes a healthy and whole human being. The book includes many of Osho's meditation methods.

Mindfulness in the Modern World
How Can I Make Meditation Part of My Everyday Life?

ABOUT OSHO

Osho's unique contribution to the understanding of who we are defies categorization. Mystic and scientist, a rebellious spirit whose sole interest is to alert humanity to the urgent need to discover a new way of living. To continue as before is to invite threats to our very survival on this unique and beautiful planet.

His essential point is that only by changing ourselves, one individual at a time, can the outcome of all our "selves" – our societies, our cultures, our beliefs, our world – also change. The doorway to that change is meditation.

Osho the scientist has experimented and scrutinized all the approaches of the past and examined their effects on the modern human being and responded to their shortcomings by creating a new starting point for the hyperactive 21st Century mind: OSHO Active Meditations.

Once the agitation of a modern lifetime has started to settle, "activity" can melt into "passivity," a key starting point of real meditation. To support this next step, Osho has transformed the ancient "art of listening" into a subtle contemporary methodology: the OSHO Talks. Here words become music, the listener discovers who is listening, and the awareness moves from what is being heard to the individual doing the listening. Magically, as silence arises, what needs to be heard is understood directly, free from the distraction of a mind that can only interrupt and interfere with this delicate process.

These thousands of talks cover everything from the individual quest for meaning to the most urgent social and political issues facing society today. Osho's books are not written but are transcribed from audio and video recordings of these extemporaneous talks to international audiences. As he puts it, "So remember: whatever I am saying is not just for you...I am talking also for the future generations."

Osho has been described by *The Sunday Times* in London as one of the "1000 Makers of the 20th Century" and by American author Tom Robbins as "the most dangerous man since Jesus Christ." *Sunday Mid-Day* (India) has selected Osho as one of ten people – along with Gandhi, Nehru and Buddha – who have changed the destiny of India.

About his own work Osho has said that he is helping to create the conditions for the birth of a new kind of human being. He often characterizes this new human being as "Zorba the Buddha" – capable both of enjoying the earthy pleasures of a Zorba the Greek and the silent serenity of a Gautama the Buddha.

Running like a thread through all aspects of Osho's talks and meditations is a vision that encompasses both the timeless wisdom of all ages past and the highest potential of today's (and tomorrow's) science and technology.

Osho is known for his revolutionary contribution to the science of inner transformation, with an approach to meditation that acknowledges the accelerated pace of contemporary life. His unique OSHO Active Meditations™ are designed to first release the accumulated stresses of body and mind, so that it is then easier to take an experience of stillness and thought-free relaxation into daily life.

Two autobiographical works by the author are available:
Autobiography of a Spiritually Incorrect Mystic,
St Martins Press, New York (book and eBook)
Glimpses of a Golden Childhood,
OSHO Media International, Pune, India (book and eBook)

OSHO INTERNATIONAL MEDITATION RESORT

Each year the Meditation Resort welcomes thousands of people from more than 100 countries. The unique campus provides an opportunity for a direct personal experience of a new way of living – with more awareness, relaxation, celebration and creativity. A great variety of around-the-clock and around-the-year program options are available. Doing nothing and just relaxing is one of them!

All of the programs are based on Osho's vision of "Zorba the Buddha" – a qualitatively new kind of human being who is able *both* to participate creatively in everyday life *and* to relax into silence and meditation.

Location
Located 100 miles southeast of Mumbai in the thriving modern city of Pune, India, the OSHO International Meditation Resort is a holiday destination with a difference. The Meditation Resort is spread over 28 acres of spectacular gardens in a beautiful tree-lined residential area.

OSHO Meditations
A full daily schedule of meditations for every type of person includes both traditional and revolutionary methods, and particularly the OSHO Active Meditations™. The daily meditation program takes place in what must be the world's largest meditation hall, the OSHO Auditorium.

OSHO Multiversity
Individual sessions, courses and workshops cover everything from creative arts to holistic health, personal transformation, relationship and life transition, transforming meditation into a lifestyle for life and work, esoteric sciences, and the "Zen" approach to sports and recreation. The secret of the OSHO Multiversity's success lies in the fact that all its programs are combined with meditation, supporting the understanding that as human beings we are far more than the sum of our parts.

OSHO Basho Spa

The luxurious Basho Spa provides for leisurely open-air swimming surrounded by trees and tropical green. The uniquely styled, spacious Jacuzzi, the saunas, gym, tennis courts...all these are enhanced by their stunningly beautiful setting.

Cuisine

A variety of different eating areas serve delicious Western, Asian and Indian vegetarian food – most of it organically grown especially for the Meditation Resort. Breads and cakes are baked in the resort's own bakery.

Night life

There are many evening events to choose from – dancing being at the top of the list! Other activities include full-moon meditations beneath the stars, variety shows, music performances and meditations for daily life.

Facilities

You can buy all of your basic necessities and toiletries in the Galleria. The Multimedia Gallery sells a large range of OSHO media products. There is also a bank, a travel agency and a Cyber Café on-campus. For those who enjoy shopping, Pune provides all the options, ranging from traditional and ethnic Indian products to all of the global brand-name stores.

Accommodation

You can choose to stay in the elegant rooms of the OSHO Guesthouse, or for longer stays on campus you can select one of the OSHO Living-In programs. Additionally there is a plentiful variety of nearby hotels and serviced apartments.

www.osho.com/meditationresort
www.osho.com/guesthouse
www.osho.com/livingin

OSHO DYNAMIC MEDITATION

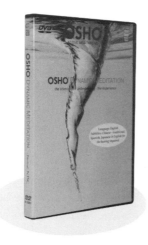

A full media experience of the revolutionary and most well-known of the Osho Active Meditation methods.

OSHO Dynamic Meditation is a one-hour meditation, with five stages.

It is a fast, intense and thorough way to break old, ingrained patterns that keep one imprisoned in the past, and to experience the freedom, the witnessing, silence and peace that are hidden behind these prison walls.

The meditation is best done in the early morning, when "the whole of nature becomes alive, the night has gone, the sun is coming up and everything becomes conscious and alert."

The DVD features:
1. OSHO Dynamic Meditation instruction video
2. From Chaos to Silence (shared experiences with this meditation)
3. OSHO Talks: Osho insights on Dynamic Meditation
4. OSHO Dynamic Meditation music with sound of participants
5. The OSHO International Meditation Resort

MORE OSHO BOOKS

Over 7000 hours of talks by Osho have been transcribed into books. If you go to www.osho.com you can sort the titles by subject so you can choose the books that interest you most.

THE BOOK OF SECRETS
112 Keys to the Mystery Within
Osho continues to inspire millions of people worldwide in their individual search for joy, fulfillment, depth, and silence. All his talks address the question of how we can live each moment of our daily lives in awareness, relaxation and totality.

In *The Book of Secrets* we are invited to experience and experiment with the games and situations that everyday life brings through the tools of our senses. The 4000 year-old *Vigyan Bhairav Tantra* is a compendium of highly condensed, telegraphic instructions for 112 different awareness techniques that bring us into the present moment. Osho describes each technique in detail, and explains how we can discover which is the best one for us and how to integrate it into our daily lives.

ISBN: 978-81-7261-217-7

THE NEW ALCHEMY: TO TURN YOU ON
Innermost Secrets of Consciousness
The New Alchemy: To Turn You On is a practical, detailed guide for those exploring meditation. Osho has a vast understanding of the steps and pitfalls along the way and the unique gift of communicating them directly and simply.

"Whenever you have found a technique, a way, retreat within, go within. Experiment with it there, in your subjectivity, in your heart. Experience it. Don't just go on thinking about what meditation is. Do it! Only then will you know what it is."

While the emphasis is on active meditation, Osho skillfully interweaves commentaries on Mabel Collins' *Light on the Path*, to further support the seeker's understanding.

ISBN: 978-81-7261-235-1

FOR MORE INFORMATION

For a full selection of OSHO multilingual online
destinations, see osho.com/allaboutosho

The official and comprehensive website of OSHO
International is osho.com

For more OSHO unique content and formats see:

- OSHO Active Meditations: osho.com/meditate
- iOSHO, a bouquet of digital OSHO experiences featuring
  OSHO Zen Tarot, TV, Library, Horoscope, eGreetings and
  Radio. Please take a moment to do a one time registration
  which will allow you a universal login. Registration is free
  and open to anyone with a valid email address:
  osho.com/iosho
- The OSHO online shop: osho.com/shop
- Visit the OSHO International Meditation Resort:
  osho.com/visit
- Contribute in the OSHO Translation Project:
  oshotalks.com
- Read the OSHO Newsletters: osho.com/NewsLetters
- Watch OSHO on YouTube:
  youtube.com/user/OSHOInternational
- Follow OSHO on Facebook:
  facebook.com/osho.international.meditation.resort
  and Twitter: twitter.com/OSHO

Thank you for buying this OSHO book.